I Am An
Angelic Walk-In

Claire Candy Hough

ANGEL HEALING HOUSE
LOS ANGELES, CA

I AM AN ANGELIC WALK-IN
Claire Candy Hough

ISBN-13: 978-0-9818576-4-0
ISBN-10: 0-9818576-4-7

Printed in the U.S.A.

First U.S. Edition: 2016

Library of Congress Control Number: 2016935078

Published by
Angel Healing House
Los Angeles, California

www.angelhealinghouse.com

Dedication

I dedicate this book to the former soul of Claire Candy,
who was in the body prior to January 2003, and to her amazing
capacity to give to others.

Acknowledgements

My life has been blessed with so many people who loved, supported, encouraged and promoted my journey as an Angel on the Earth plane.

I have such profound gratitude for Val Odgers-Jewell and Robyn Anderson for looking after me in the crucial six-month period after I walked in, when I had no idea of what had happened to me. Thank you for feeding my anorexic frame, and nourishing my physical form with food and my emotional wellbeing with a sisterly friendship of concern, caring, love and devotion.

I am forever grateful to my Reiki Master/Teacher Diane McCormick for providing me with not only physical nourishment and inviting me for countless dinners, but also for the spiritual nourishment of my soul, and initiating and attuning me to the wonders of Reiki.

A HUGE thank you to my Earth angel sister Donna-May Krumbholz for following her inspired intuition to invite me to her 'Come as Your Favourite Rock Star' engagement party even though she had just met me, providing the Divine moment for Stevie Nicks to meet Elvis.

I would like to send enormous, heartfelt thanks to my dear Dragon friend Patrick Moore who was the first to confirm to me that I indeed had had an Angelic Walk-In experience. We have done this dance of help, love and devotion through many incarnations as Dragons and Angels are the best of friends!

I am eternally grateful to my beautiful friends and healing practitioner colleagues on the Sunshine Coast of Queensland, Australia: Jean Sheehan, Lynn Barrett, and Therese Pettiford-Brudell. Each of you supported and promoted my business, Angel Healing House, and in addition provided loving encouragement for me to blossom and grow as a healing practitioner.

A huge debt of gratitude goes to my lovely friend Lesley

Nicholson for providing me with a work space to see clients for the five months that Pete and I were forced to remain in Wollongong, NSW, while waiting for his green card to come through. Thank you, dear friend, for your generosity and kindness of spirit in promoting me.

Immense gratitude also goes to Lisa Noland-Shalofsky for all your support, promotion, encouragement and all the beautiful angel messages that you provided, giving me guidance and clarity along my journey.

Thank you to my dear spiritual family in Los Angeles who have provided such wonderful support and love as I have traversed this physical world:

to David Matthew Brown for your invaluable love, support and encouragement and for our many spiritual discussions and meetings over countless cups of tea and coffee;

to my dear friends Beth Fortman-Brand and Doug Brand. Your generosity, love and kindness that you have shown Pete and me have been such an enormous gift and blessing in our lives;

to my beautiful kindred soul sister, Kristie Reeves, for sharing and promoting my work;

and to my dear friend John Romeo, for all our yummy, shared brunches and for your love, guidance, encouragement and channeled messages that have provided me with great clarity and insights along my journey.

And, finally, to my wonderful husband Pete, who felt the hand of God on his back only five days after meeting me, and heard God's words, "Ask her to marry you;" thank you for listening and asking.

Preface

I woke up from my nightmare at the age of forty-seven-and-a-half.

For the first time in my life, I gave myself permission to honor my thoughts and feelings. By acknowledging and respecting who I was, I began to transform the negative and predictable way in which I had previously responded and reacted my entire life. It was the realization that, 'it is not what happens to us in life, but our perception of what happens' that made all the difference. After all, two people can have the same experience and one can choose to see it as a blessing, while another sees it as a tragedy.

I understood for the first time that it was only by letting go of my negative thought patterns and destructive habits, and replacing them with positive choices, that I could escape the chains of low self-worth, blame and judgment.

I turned my life around by choosing to love myself, but not from an egotistical, arrogant or selfish point of view. I allowed myself to emulate the beauty, power and magnificence that was and is my Divine inherent birthright. By acknowledging and recognizing the Divine within me, I stopped the perpetuation of self-sabotaging behaviors, fully allowing my Divinity to shine and radiate forth.

The good news is that this Divinity is not solely within a select few for them to be lauded, praised or revered, as it is within each and every one of us. The more we emulate these qualities, the more our lives begin to reflect the peace, happiness and joy that we feel within.

We wake up from our own particular nightmare when we decide that the pain and suffering we are choosing to hang on to and perpetuate doesn't serve us any more. Once we make this decision, we can begin to make steps towards being proactive with our lives, making positive change, rather than merely being reactionary.

In other words, we simply choose to be happy.

The amazing realization is that each and every one of us has this magnificence inside us and the same ability to radiate an inner light, which transcends our chosen physical appearance. By opening up to our intuition and following our heart's desires, we allow our lives to flow freely, no longer allowing external cues to dominate and rule our world. By loving yourself, you start to experience life through the eyes of a child with all its wonder, enchantment and magic.

Through my healing practice, Angel Healing House, I have often said to my clients that we teach best what we need to learn most. The foundation of my practice is loving, honoring and respecting ourselves. It was only by becoming an independent, loving person on my own, that I could then go on to truly love another without depending on them for my own happiness.

By connecting to the light of our Divine eternal nature, our realities start to reflect that inner radiance, as we have given ourselves permission to shine.

But for the majority of my life, this was not the case.

For forty-seven years, I had experienced a life in which my every thought and action was to please others; as I had completely forgotten the importance of who I was and had turned off my inner light. Age, in this case, is not a determinant as to when or if a person decides to 'wake-up' to their Divine light. We each have been blessed with free will to make choices and decisions in life at any stage along our journey.

Throughout all of human existence on our beloved planet Earth, humans have learned through the telling of stories. Whether they were sitting around campfires under a star-filled sky or huddling for warmth in caves on a frosty night, coming together in a traditional ceremony or reading an exciting tale or fable, the information in the story so often confirms what they already know deep within and gives them direction and courage to follow their hearts.

It is amazing that when we are ready to receive the information, either the book or the person with the story to tell will appear in our lives. It is often by hearing that particular person's story, and how they turned their life around, that we gather information on how we can possibly improve our own lives.

I hope that, in the re-telling of my story, it will inspire others to give themselves permission to shine and start to fashion a beautiful life for themselves.

Love and Angel Blessings,
Claire Candy Hough/Angel Ariel

Introduction

Looking back at the canvas of my life, I have painted countless faces and situations into my daily routines. Standing up close to my life's design, I can perceive very different impressions depending on which part I choose to focus. There are particular areas of the painting that are bright and shining. Looking at these events, one can almost feel the gleeful, unbridled joy shared amongst family and friends. If one only sees this part of the canvas, one could imagine a charmed life.

Yet the impression changes considerably when one stands in front of other areas, such as divorce, illness, financial ruin and disappointment. The life then takes on a dark, troubled, even desperate feeling.

It is only by taking a step back and viewing the picture of one's life as a whole that one can get a better sense of the meaning of that life. In viewing the bigger picture from this wider perspective, we are able to discern the interplay between the happy, lighter moments of our lives and the dark, challenging times. Often, it is from a distance that our perception starts to change and we can appreciate why we made certain choices, and how they either served our growth and development or stunted it. Waking up to this appreciation in January 2003, I started to view my life very differently.

Through new eyes, I could now clearly see that all the people and situations that I had drawn into the picture of my life were helping me learn my most important lessons: to respect who I am, to be independent and to love myself. Take note that not everyone's lessons are the same. With this grander perspective on my life, even though I now choose to rejoice that I drew certain people and events to my experience, this feeling of celebration was not always the case.

For the majority of my life, I felt sorry for myself because I chose to put more importance on other people's opinions than on my own. Languishing as I looked out of the bars of a prison cell of my own making, my life was a constant replay of diminishing who I was as I hungered to be nourished and validated by others. And when individuals obtain their sense of self-worth from external sources, instead of from their own loving center, then they are continually vulnerable. With no self-created, loving, secure foundation to anchor the strings of my life, I acted as a marionette, continually allowing myself to be manipulated and danced around at the whim and discretion of others. In essence, my whole life was spent looking for the love and respect that was within me the entire time.

I now know that it is only by nourishing and nurturing ourselves and embracing our Divine eternal nature that the rest of our lives will flow with ease and grace.

Come with me on a journey back in time and experience a life filled with well thought out, expertly contracted and precisely timed challenges that helped one soul grow and another soul to create Heaven on Earth.

Love and Angel Blessings,
Claire Candy Hough/Angel Ariel

Who?

by Leonard Milgraum

Who are you and who am I?
Separate pieces of a pie,
Each unique a special soul,
Yet mesh and meld to form one whole.

Who are you and who am I?
Puzzle parts that mystify,
Hidden hints, clever clues,
Part of every rainbow's hues,

Each a ripple in a stream,
Each a part of someone's dream,
Each a shimmer of the sun,
A precious piece of everyone,

A glimmer of the Golden Rule,
An ever changing molecule,
Each a bit of he and she,
Ultimate geometry,

Part and parcel of this verse,
Partners in the Universe,
Each a portion of the sum,
Each a journey to become.

Can you fathom who you are?
Part of every shining star,
Part of every mother's birth,
Part of all that's on this Earth.

Then who am I and who are you?
The question serves as answer too.
All combine to form the 'we'
That's part of God's eternity.

Chapters

I Am An
Angelic Walk-In

1

Choosing a Physical Incarnation

Returning to the transition level of Heaven was very different this time for Angel Ariel. With her advanced spiritual knowledge, she was able to easily bypass the usual encounters that souls experience as they cross over from the illusions of Earth's physical realm to their one true home in Spirit.

She didn't need to see deceased relatives at a homecoming party to know where she had arrived. Nor did she need to review her Earthly incarnation at the Hall of Justice in order to understand the effect that her words, actions and thoughts had had on her life and the lives of others. She didn't even need to meet with the wise Etheric Council in the Hall of Akashic Records, as she had fully awakened to her Divine eternal nature. With her free will, Angel Ariel knew full well that it was she who would determine what was going to happen next.

While pondering this decision, she chose to go somewhere beautiful to help provide some much-needed inspiration. As all thought forms in Heaven present instant manifestation, Angel Ariel immediately found herself in the verdant hanging gardens surrounding the Hall of Wisdom. One could not help but be inspired by the beauty of the cascading waterfalls and the vivid colors of the endless varieties of flowers and plants. Resting on one of the carved benches in the courtyard, she breathed in the floral scents and allowed her attention to settle upon her heart. For it was in her heart that she knew she would find all the answers to her questions.

Searching her innermost feelings, she recalled the joy of working on Heaven's different creative levels between previous incarnations. A smile crept across her face as she recalled composing with the towering musical giants, Bach and Mozart. As egos are not a part of Heaven's domain, her musical talents were also acknowledged and recognized along with these gifted souls.

As much as she had enjoyed composing, she also loved painting. Angel Ariel recalled that she had spent her time between physical incarnations drawing a series of wonderful Italian landscapes in honor of her beloved Tuscan villa. Yet, because of the enormous changes within her, none of these previous pursuits made her heart sing.

Struggling with deciding where to go next, she thought back to how each physical incarnation had helped her to advance along the spiritual path. In answer to her thoughts, holographic images of her former incarnations immediately appeared. Silently observing them, she watched scenes of her lives as an Egyptian princess, a healer in 14th century Scotland, a Venetian courtesan in 16th century Italy, a young girl captured off the coast of Africa and forced into a life of slavery, along with her life as a revered member of the Native American Lakota tribe.

She remembered that some of these lives were so harrowing that all she wanted to do was to escape to the familiar comfort of her heavenly homes to rest and restore her energies and indulge in her creative passions. Yet, instead of wishing to forget the challenges of her previous lives, she now felt a great sense of pride for the choices that she had made and the lessons that she had learned. It was the reconnection to her spiritual wisdom that saw her graduate to being of angelic service and freeing herself from the birth and death cycle of incarnating back to Earth in physical form. Embracing every aspect of her former lives, Angel Ariel felt an excited urge to serve in a very new way.

A brightly colored butterfly lit gently upon her arm and brought her back into the present moment. She smiled at this wonderful sign of confirmation, knowing that butterflies signify transformation. Angel Ariel knew deep in her heart that the challenges and struggles of each one of her past incarnations were beautifully crafted stepping stones that were vastly important to where she now found herself. With all the spiritual knowledge that she had obtained from these incarnations, it suddenly dawned on her in which capacity she most wanted to serve.

Instantly, she began to imagine herself as a spiritual teacher to other souls in Heaven. As if in confirmation, she heard a beautiful chorus of angels' voices softly floating on the breeze. And the more she focused her attention on this inspired excitement within her heart, the more her thoughts began to paint themselves into her reality.

Far beyond any ordinary red brick schoolhouse, Angel Ariel's imagination and heartfelt desires began to paint a wonderful sanctuary of learning, with the glories of nature as its walls and the sky as its ceiling. Benches and desks appeared, surrounded by leafy, green trees as the sounds of birds filled her classroom. Proudly admiring her handiwork, Angel Ariel voiced out loud, "Now all I need are my students."

From that moment on, Angel Ariel would teach spiritual law to thousands of souls as they returned from their physical lives to their one true home in Spirit. Although it was not compulsory to attend spiritual schooling in Heaven, most souls hungered for answers to questions concerning their lives spent on the Earth plane.

As the sun broke through the canopy of leaves above her classroom, Angel Ariel waited for another group of assembled students to settle down before beginning class. Yet, there was one man who was anything but patient as he frantically waved his arms in order to be chosen. Announcing to her students that the topic for today's class would be Responsibility, she selected the impatient gentleman. Standing respectfully, he said, "My name is Paul. I still can't understand it. I tried so hard in my last life to be responsible. I worked hard and spent long hours at the law firm where I was a partner. I made lots of money for my family, and provided everything that they could have wanted. Yet, even though I was responsible, my wife still left me. She was the reason for my heart attack. Angel Ariel, could you explain why this could have possibly happened?"

Angel Ariel smiled, as she knew the answers to her students' questions long before they posed them. Yet, she patiently answered each question with such individualized care and attention that every student felt as if their question had been presented for the very first time.

And while Angel Ariel was a compassionate teacher, she was completely honest with her students. As far as she was concerned, their spiritual advancement was of great importance and she took their enlightenment very seriously. It was her dedication and devotion to living God's will that had brought her to the position of Spiritual Master Teacher.

Drawing her attention back to her waiting student, Angel Ariel replied, "We in Heaven applaud you, dear Paul. From the transcripts of your life, it is obvious that you took responsibility by physically providing for the needs of your family. Yet for the most part, it does appear that you were emotionally absent." Pausing a moment to find just the right words, Angel Ariel continued, "It did seem that, as each of your job positions provided more and more money, your ego grew larger and your priorities changed dramatically as you climbed the ladder of success. Perhaps you put all your efforts into your career and forgot about your family?"

True to his profession, Paul was just about to defend his case when a holographic screen suddenly appeared and began to present examples of Paul's absentee life. Squirming uncomfortably in his seat, he watched scenes of being absent from his wife's and children's lives. He watched year after year of missed birthday parties, school concerts and plays, parent-teacher conferences, and medical emergencies that his wife had to attend alone. In addition to his physical absence from the family, his decision to work long, grueling hours caused him to become emotionally unavailable, judgmental and abusive.

Stopping the projection, Angel Ariel calmly stated, "For every action there is a reaction. Whatever you sow, ye shall reap. This is but one of the eternal spiritual laws that have an effect on what ultimately occurs in our lives. Continually throughout your marriage, Paul, your wife made it very clear to you that she loved you dearly and solely wished for you to be more involved in your children's lives and to make your relationship with her a priority. For twenty-two years, through your free will and free choice, Paul, you placed your work above your family."

As the holographic depiction showed his wife leaving him, Angel Ariel continued, "In the end, after almost three decades of marriage, your wife simply got tired of telling you that she wanted to be shown that she was as important as your work. As her wishes and desires were shown no respect, she simply left to find someone who would make her emotional needs a priority."

As there is no blame, shame nor judgment in Heaven, Paul nodded his head in agreement, as he finally understood his lack of responsibility towards the health of his marriage. Walking over and putting her hand on Paul's shoulder, Angel Ariel said, "With this greater understanding of responsibility, tell us what you learned from that lesson."

Paul hesitantly smiled and said, "I learned that if I want to receive the love, the caring and the respect from others, I have to be responsible for embracing and living those qualities first within me." With a chuckle and a slight smile, Paul added, "I guess I really did lose balance in my life and gave money and power all my attention."

With a wise smile, Angel Ariel replied, "Well stated. Yet, it is not just in the theory of knowledge that we advance spiritually. Knowledge for knowledge's sake is quite empty when it is not put into practice. This is why, Paul, you will have the choice to select opportunities in your next life to show that you really have understood the concept of responsibility that we have spoken about today."

Angel Ariel asked the class to review and discuss their notes in groups. She smiled as she recalled the many examples of protestations that former students gave to defend their choices in their physical incarnations. One soul had told her, "It was my wife's fault that I slept with her best friend. If she had not gone back to work and neglected me then I would not have had to find comfort in the arms of another woman."

Another soul had rationalized, "Sure, I skimmed money off the books at work, but anyone else would have done the same thing. The boss was so mean and paid us so little that I had to do something to get even."

No matter how sincerely the souls protested, Angel Ariel remained impartial about the details of each life. She was able to compassionately and honestly demonstrate that by having chosen to live a life of honor, respect and responsibility, the soul's life would have been a reflection of those same qualities.

She adored her life as a Spiritual Teacher and was commended many times by the Etheric Council for her wonderful, caring work. What she loved best about her teaching position was that each class was different, as new souls were always arriving. And, although she was an impartial teacher and tried very hard not to play favorites, occasionally a student would appear who would touch her heart in quite a profound way.

Sitting under a bright, blue sky, Angel Ariel waited patiently for a new group of souls to learn under her tutelage. As the students began to gather, she scanned the eager faces and saw one soul that caught her attention. Sitting in the back of the class was a girl with olive skin and flowing dark hair. Tuning into the girl's energy, Angel Ariel knew her name was Claire and she could clearly intuit that she was a very young soul. Young, untried souls who have not incarnated back to Earth, had not experienced the practical benefits of learning from many hard won battles or gained wisdom through character-building challenges and struggles.

Over time, the shy, young beauty was captivated by Angel Ariel's loving, compassionate manner as she listened intently to her sage advice. It wasn't long before Claire moved from the back row up to the front and she became a more vocal participant in class discussions. She especially loved it when Angel Ariel would share details about the stories of her various physical incarnations back on Earth and the lessons that she had learned.

Claire would be riveted to Angel Ariel's every word as she described her life of privilege and wealth in ancient Egypt. She made notes as Angel Ariel drew parallels between the spiritual lessons she garnered from her incarnations as a healer in 14th century Scotland and her life as a Lakota native. Claire became so taken with Angel Ariel that she would often stay after class, seeking to learn greater spiritual wisdom. And every time, Angel Ariel would patiently answer Claire's seemingly endless questions with compassionate guidance.

Yet, Angel Ariel felt in her heart that no matter how much learning Claire received, it would never be a substitute for the practical application of the knowledge. From her own journey, she knew that one learns best by experience, rather than by just theorizing. Over her long teaching career, she had witnessed many souls who knew spiritual law back to front, as they spent countless hours in debates and discussions. Yet, many of these souls were too frightened to test their spiritual knowledge by choosing to learn their lessons in the hardest arena of all – through a physical incarnation on planet Earth.

Recalling her own incarnations, she thought, "It's very easy to experience an emotion like love and faith in Heaven when all around you are expressing these beautiful qualities. Yet, it is vastly different to actually put yourself in a position where you have to try to find love and faith in the challenges of duality where none so often exists." She knew what it felt like to have her faith tested when she experienced hatred and bigotry in her former lives.

From her work as a Spiritual Teacher, she saw that the majority of souls had an overwhelming sense of pride in just having completed their time on Earth; even if they didn't fully learn all the lessons that they had set out to accomplish.

Knowing all this, Angel Ariel could not force Claire to experience life on Earth, as one cannot interfere with free will. What she could do was to speak of her own experiences and how those incarnations enriched her more than she could ever have imagined. Class after class, Angel Ariel painted the wonderful imagery of contrasts that were an integral part of her physical incarnations. With each new class, Claire began to entertain the thought of physical incarnation to further her own spiritual growth.

It was not long after that Claire told Angel Ariel that she had made the decision to experience her first incarnation. Angel Ariel praised her for her courage and willingness to open herself to new challenges and growth along her spiritual path. Once the decision had been made, Claire did not want to waste any time and excitedly told Angel Ariel that she was leaving to meet with the Etheric Council. Angel Ariel asked if she could walk with her to the Hall of Akashic Records. As they made their way along the winding path to the hall, Angel Ariel took Claire's hand and smiled wisely.

"Remember, Claire, that no matter what happens, you have all the ancient wisdom within yourself. All you have to do to access this wisdom is to look inside. Know that you will never be alone as your angelic help is always with you offering protection and guidance." As the path ended in front of the great hall, Claire hugged Angel Ariel and thanked her for all her help. With teacher's pride, she watched Claire walk up the marble steps.

Entering the huge hall, Claire saw the Etheric Council appear in front of her. Upon seeing her face, the semi-circle of twelve wise Elders looked up over their glasses and communicated through their hearts.

"Hello, dear Claire. We are delighted that you have decided to step forward for your first incarnation on Earth." Smiling tenderly, the Elders opened up her Book of Life and picked up a long quill pen. "Now then, Claire, who will be your choice for your parents?" At the realization that she would actually have to participate in writing the contract for her Earthly incarnation, Claire panicked at the question and froze. She quickly remembered Angel Ariel's physical lives and the characteristics of her different family members.

Taking a deep breath, she told the Council that she wanted her mother to exhibit the fiery determination and will of Angel Ariel's mother, Catherina, when she had lived her incarnation as Angelica, a courtesan in Venice, Italy. And, quickly remembering Angel Ariel's incarnation as one of the Lakota and the way that they had lived in harmony with the land, she then added that she also wanted her mother to have this same deep connection with nature.

The Etheric Council smiled, as they knew that Claire was copying what she had learned from the incarnations of her beloved teacher. But the Council did not say anything, as they knew that we all have to start from somewhere and that copying is the highest form of flattery. The final trait that Claire wanted for her mother to demonstrate was the gift of prophecy, just like Annabel Rose's mother had passed down to her in Angel Ariel's incarnation as a healer in 14th century Scotland.

Pausing between writing notes and keeping pace with Claire's desires, the Etheric Council said, "By combining all these traits, your mother will be an extraordinary woman." Suddenly there was shared laughter amongst these sage Elders. "Claire, your father will have to be someone very special to hold a candle to such a strong lady." Once again, Claire thought back to Angel Ariel's incarnations.

With conviction, she replied, "I want my father to have the same passion and zest for life as Angel Ariel's dear faerie friend Violet. In this way, he will always remind me to be childlike and joyful. In addition, I wish him to have the same characteristics as Wachinksapa, the medicine man. He displayed a profound spiritual connection to God and an ability to be in the world but not of it. My mother and father will have this spiritual connection and great love for nature."

The Elders looked up from the page and chuckled. "We are very impressed with your choices, Claire, for they seem to be a match made in Heaven, if you pardon the expression."

Claire then went on to describe her three brothers. Her eldest brother would exemplify the characteristics of Aknatan, the slave boy whom Angel Ariel had known in her life in Egypt. He would be strong in his convictions and stand up for any injustices with a determined will. Claire decided that her two younger brothers would demonstrate the beautiful qualities of the Native American boy Ohiyesha, whom the medicine man had taught. Both her brothers would be highly intelligent, soft-spoken, and have a deep connection to God.

Having carefully painted a vivid picture of her Earth family, the wise Elders asked Claire what she wanted to achieve in this lifetime. With this being her first incarnation, she had not given any thought as to what lessons she wanted to learn. Having seen this many times before, the Etheric Council was quick to give her some helpful advice.

"While you are deciding, Claire, may we suggest that the best way that you can be of service to others, is if you are of service to yourself? By honoring your gifts and talents and doing what you love doing, your energy will be so high and abundant that it will greatly affect all other energies."

Taking some time to ponder the answer to this very important question, Claire replied, "In this lifetime, I want to love myself, realize God's creative expression in me, be independent and shine my Divine light." She then paused and hesitantly added, "May I ask to keep my telepathic and psychic gifts?"

This was a question that the Etheric Council was very used to hearing from young souls who had never experienced a physical incarnation. And even though the Elders knew that they wished to make their physical incarnation easier, they also knew that all choices not only had their advantages, but disadvantages as well. As in countless other cases, they longed to say, "Be mindful of what you ask for." Instead, they merely stated, "You have free will, Claire. If that is what you want to experience, then it will be so."

Pondering this part of her contract, Claire had difficulty imagining that beautiful souls who loved her so deeply could ever play the part of someone who would try to disrespect or hurt her. Knowing that many times our most important lessons come in hardship and adversity, she carefully chose these souls' characteristics to be in direct contrast to her own. Furrowing her brow, she chose two men who, by their actions and self-centered natures, would create great pain within her. Over time, her profound sadness would create the impetus for the need to change and to make forward movement in her life. Once the contract of her physical incarnation was written, the Elders were just about to close her Book of Life, when Claire quickly shouted, "Stop! I almost forgot to include the beautiful experience of having children."

She decided to choose a dark-haired beauty for her first-born girl, just like Angel Ariel's description of Angelica in her days as a courtesan. Willful and independent, she would have a great hunger and love for books and education. Next, she chose to have a son. Like her brothers, he would also have the soft, gentle qualities of Ohiyesha, the Lakota boy who was apprenticed to the wise medicine man. In addition, Claire chose for her son to have the magical power of higher perception like those of Adetoun's beloved Shaman from Angel Ariel's life in Africa.

As she completed her choices, the Elders said, "We must conclude our meeting by stating that what you have written in your Book of Life is your next journey. The most important part of a life is not the outline, but the decisions that you choose to make during that lifetime. Because you have free will, remember that the course of your destination can be changed in any given moment. To help the path of your life flow with greater ease, always respect and honor yourself, follow your heart and never let anyone take your power away."

Claire and the Etheric Council then signed her contract. Closing her Book of Life, the Elders stood, bowed and wished her a wonderful journey.

In an instant, she found herself standing on the transition platform as she waited to visit Earth for the very first time. When it was finally her turn to step forward, she panicked, hesitated and began to step back. Angel Ariel appeared by her side. "Claire, I will be your Guardian Angel to guide and protect you. Know that I am always with you." She kissed Claire on the forehead. "Go with God's blessings." Claire then stepped forward into the tunnel and was instantly pulled into the physical dimension of Earth.

2

Far, Far from Home

Crawling close to the corner of her enclosure, she grasped the bars and pulled herself up on shaky legs. The soft, cool molding on the edge of the crib prompted the baby to open her mouth and gum the smooth, plastic lining. Her eyes smiled and twinkled as she watched the familiar, non-physical beings smiling back at her. She explained telepathically to the angels that, although she was living with a very nice family, she had decided to return to her one true home in Heaven. As lovingly as possible, her angels gently conveyed, *"This is your home now, for you chose it to be so, in this physical incarnation."*

Upon hearing their words, the toddler's lip began to quiver as a huge burden of reality weighed heavily on the little girl's heart. Trembling uncontrollably, her tiny legs could not support her sadness any longer as she slumped down into the corner of the crib. Pools of tears began to well in her pretty, blue eyes and stream down her cheeks as she watched her beloved angels wave goodbye and fade from view. With the feeling of abandonment crushing down upon her tiny shoulders and the realization that she was here to stay, the little girl buried her head in her blanket and cried herself to sleep.

Unlike most souls who have their psychic abilities veiled in a human incarnation, Claire had asked to retain them. With her request granted by the Etheric Council, it meant that she was born with the ability to see, hear and communicate with non-physical beings. Instead of making her life easier, the constant reminder of her home in Heaven made it devastatingly difficult to adjust to a physical life. This one request created a deep longing in her heart to return to her one true home across the veil. Her clear connection to Spirit became a constant weight on her soul and made her doubt that she could endure the experience of a human life. Her difficulty in adjusting fully to life on Earth lead her to live as if she was always on the edge of life looking in.

Claire Candy was named after her mother's mother, Grandmother Clara, who had died of tuberculosis when Candy's mother, Sylvia, was only two-and-a-half years old. Clara had the gift of prophecy and had handed this gift down to her only child. With Sylvia being born in Romania, there was an undeniable gypsy connection and the ability to foretell the future ran in the family. And although there were many eerie coincidences of Candy's mother knowing events before they happened, the subject of actually being clairvoyant was never discussed.

The 'Candy' part of her name came from a famous pin-up model in the 1950s named Candy Jones. This very popular model would go on to lead a hidden life which was later associated with conspiracy theories. In the book *The CIA's Control of Candy Jones,* the author Donald Bain describes how Candy Jones was brainwashed by the CIA to act as a courier as part of its mind control program.

Strange that Claire Candy was named after Candy Jones, as she would also allow her sense of self to be erased by denying her Divine light within. In doing so, she did the very thing that the Etheric Council told her not to do, which was to give her power away. Ultimately, her choice to hide her spiritual gifts would lead to her completely forgetting who she was.

As she grew older and her clairvoyant and clairaudient gifts became stronger, Candy felt terribly alone and very different from others. Constantly feeling unsettled in her Earthly incarnation, she became determined to stay connected to her angelic guides. Adopting a dreamy, quiet nature, she often appeared as if she was 'off with the faeries.' In fact, her sense of being in the world, yet not of it, did not go unnoticed by her father. He often said, "When you would speak to Candy, it seemed like imaginary shutters came down over her eyes, as if she wasn't even there." He commented that her nature reminded him of the lyrics of the title song from the movie *Midnight Cowboy* that he used to sing to her. *"Everybody's talking at me, I don't hear a word they're saying, Only the echoes of my mind. People stop and stare; I don't see their faces, only the shadows of their eyes."*

Rarely engaging with the world, she kept her interactions with the human plane to a minimum and remained in the familiar company of her angels. Yet, one of the unwritten entries in the contract of our physical incarnations is that people must be grounded in order to fully experience all the complexities of what it truly means to be a human. Some of the best lessons we learn can only be experienced in challenging circumstances that cause us pain, sorrow, loss and despair. These lessons and emotions make us stronger, help us to grow and so often force us to make much-needed forward movement in our lives.

However, the last thing that little Candy wanted to be was grounded, as she proceeded to float just above the radar of life. And while being 'off with the angels' did make her feel better, the effects of not being grounded began to interfere with her reality, as she experienced in a preschool accident.

It was a normal day during kindergarten recess and, unlike the other children who were happily playing together, Candy chose to be with her unseen friends in a far-off corner of the playground. The school bell rang, alerting the children to line up near the flagpole. Being lost in communication with her non-physical friends, Candy failed to hear the bell. Finally hearing her name being called, she looked up to see the teacher impatiently waving for her to join her classmates who were already in line. Terribly embarrassed, she ran to join the others. As she got close to the flagpole, her feet skidded across loose gravel, causing her to fall forward and hit her forehead directly on the sharp corner of the cement block.

Crumpling to the ground, she immediately became aware of a strange whirring sound, as if hundreds of bees were trapped inside her head. She then rose above her body and stared down at herself.

While Candy was trying to figure out how she could be seeing herself from this viewpoint, she was sucked into a dark tunnel with a bright, white light shining off in the distance. Upon seeing this white light, an unseen force picked her up and moved her towards it. As this force brought her to the end of the tunnel, a figure was standing in the light to greet her. She was relieved to see that it was her Grandmother Clara walking towards her. Running into her grandmother's arms, Candy was overjoyed and hugged her tightly. The immediate recognition of her grandmother was very strange, as she had died when Candy's mother was only two-and-a-half years of age; twenty-four years before Candy was born. And even though she had never met her grandmother, she instantly recognized her. Taking Candy by the hand, Clara motioned for her to kneel down on what seemed to be a cloud.

As they both peered over the edge, Candy saw lots of people surrounding a little girl who lay crumpled and unconscious on the ground with a dark burgundy pool of blood forming around her head. Snuggling closer to her grandmother, Candy thought, rather smugly, "Those people are very kind to help that poor little girl, but I am okay because I am with my grandmother."

Clearly hearing her granddaughter's thoughts, Grandmother Clara affectionately spoke to her in a sweet, yet firm voice. "You know, Claire, it is not your time to come to us yet, and you must go back."

On hearing these words, Candy felt a sinking pain in her heart, knowing that she would not be allowed to remain with her grandmother in Heaven. She did not want to return to Earth and leave her real home once more. Her Grandmother Clara then said, "I love you, Claire. One day we shall all be together again." As Clara kissed her forehead, Candy suddenly woke up in the doctor's office as the last few stitches were being sewn into her head.

On returning from this near-death experience, Candy attempted to tell others about her reunion with her Grandmother Clara. Her parents dismissed their daughter's strange recollections as being the after-effects of hitting her head and they didn't seem at all comfortable when she spoke about her experience. Patting her on the back, they told her not to worry because she would return to being 'normal' again soon. Feeling unsupported, Candy stopped speaking up for herself. It would be her inability to communicate her true feelings and acknowledge her psychic gifts that would haunt her for the next forty-five years.

After the near-death experience, she just accepted the fact that she was not normal. She rationalized that she would become a good actress and just pretend to be like everyone else.

Angel Ariel immediately felt Claire's saddened energies as her student resigned to hide her psychic gifts and remain silent. Remembering that Claire wrote in the contract before incarnating that she had intended to speak up for herself and be empowered, Angel Ariel knew all too well that, since she did not learn to speak about her psychic abilities, the lesson would be presented again at a later stage in order for her to learn it.

And even though Candy longed to return across the veil, her human incarnation certainly had many wonderful aspects. By choosing parents who loved her, an older brother and a nice house in the suburbs, she had painted a loving portrait of her childhood.

Yet, no matter how much we may desire for our lives to remain the same, it is only by experiencing change that we expand our horizons. And although all of life is a learning experience, there are significant events that occur that seem to completely change the course of peoples' lives. By far the most significant event that would change her family's lives forever was the birth of her younger brother.

As the decade of the 1960s began, Candy's younger brother, Randy, was born severely asthmatic and there were many times that her parents thought they might lose him. Placing all her trust in the medical profession, her mother ran from doctor to doctor in hopes of finding a cure for her son's debilitating condition. After receiving many conflicting diagnoses and very little helpful information (one doctor insisted that her son was simply allergic to her), Sylvia discovered that her child was highly allergic to cow's milk. It was at this point that her mother started to research natural, holistic alternatives. Through her diligence and tenacity to improve her son's life, she discovered that her young son could tolerate goat's milk. As health food stores were few and far between in the early 1960s, Candy's parents decided to raise their own goats.

Their desire to improve the family's health was in perfect alignment with Divine timing as her parents had become increasingly dissatisfied with the claustrophobia of the suburbs; they longed for a life in the country. Her brother's illness became the impetus to make this change, which set the family on a very different path.

This life change entailed her family moving to an historic home on a beautiful, forested property on Long Island Sound, New York. They purchased the property from the Mueller family, who had built a spaghetti empire. Their love of pasta was reflected in the name of the property, *Seldoon*, which is 'noodles' spelled backwards! The family shared the gently undulating hills and flowing brook with resident deer, squirrels, skunks and the usual array of animals that had already made their home in the North American forest. The historic stone and wood home had been built into the side of a hill as protection from Native American attacks in the 1700s. Candy and her brothers collected the arrowheads that were scattered throughout the forests.

Angel Ariel made note of Claire's choice of homes and locations that she had written into her contract. It was clear that Claire had chosen to experience a life surrounded by the energies of Native Americans, similar to Angel Ariel's experience as a member of the Lakota.

Not long after settling into her new home, seven-year-old Candy sensed that her family was not alone. On entering the rooms that had their walls embedded in the side of the hill, she could clearly see Native American spirits who were still connected to the land. Their filmy apparitions hovered in mid-air and grinned at her. Even though she had become accustomed to seeing angels, this was very disconcerting, as she was now starting to see souls who had crossed over. This was the so-called 'straw that broke the camel's back.' She tried on many occasions to tell her parents what she was experiencing.

Contending with her four-year-old asthmatic son and a newborn, along with managing the farm property, Sylvia had very little time left over to hear nonsense about seeing dead people or angels or whatever else her daughter's vivid imagination could conjure up. With her visions continuing to be ignored, Candy became so disheartened that she chose to spend as much time as she could outside of the house.

Looking down from Heaven, Angel Ariel watched as Claire sat by the flowing brook in deep conversation with the faeries. Having monitored every aspect of Claire's life, Angel Ariel picked up the heaviness that burdened the young girl's heart. It seemed that the outwardly assertive girl whom Angel Ariel had known from her class was now content to take a back seat and remain a silent observer of life. Angel Ariel knew that Claire would have many opportunities presented to her in order to learn the important lesson of honoring herself. In fact, her next opportunity to learn the lesson of being authentic and truthful would come when she started school.

With her parents' decision to relocate to an isolated country property, it didn't afford them many choices when it came time for Candy's education. They were fortunate that there was one school very close to their farm. And this is how their daughter became the only Jewish child at a Catholic school.

Candy did not realize that, with each contrast she brought to her life, it gave her another great opportunity to embrace being unique. But when you're a young child, all you want is to be like everyone else. Knowing that she had succeeded in hiding her clairvoyant abilities, she decided also to conceal the fact that she was Jewish in order to blend in with her surroundings.

Not long after her enrolment in the Catholic school, the family received some unexpected visitors. Answering a knock at the door, her mother was greeted by two nuns in their long, flowing habits. Introducing themselves as Candy's teachers, the nuns asked if they could come in and discuss their new pupil. They praised Candy for being such a lovely, quiet child and they hoped to see the family at mass the following Sunday.

With a very surprised look, Sylvia politely explained to the nuns that their family was Jewish. Rather bewildered, the nuns told her mother that they were led to believe otherwise.

After much embarrassment, the nuns left and Candy's mother called her into the room. She then asked how the nuns could have possibly arrived at this misconception. Shifting nervously from side to side, Candy explained that at the first assembly, the Monsignor had asked for all the Protestant children to put their hands up; which was the majority of the room. He then asked for the Catholic children to raise their hands. Trying to save herself from receiving a scolding, Candy told her mother that the Catholic children were so out-numbered that she was just trying to help even things up. Unfortunately, the spanking that she received for lying was testament that her explanation was not favorably met and carried no weight.

Aside from the religion, there was one part of her Catholic education that Candy absolutely loved. As her parents were just starting to live in a more holistic and organic way, items like cow's milk and store-bought cookies became things of the past. But as part of her new daily school routine, the nuns provided the children with milk and cookies. HALLELUJAH!

Yet there was one catch. This Heavenly snack could only be eaten after one of the students had recited *The Lord's Prayer* aloud. As the majority of the prayers in synagogue were recited in Hebrew, *The Lord's Prayer* was unfamiliar to her. The nuns chose the students in alphabetical order to recite the 'cookie prayer,' as Candy now referred to it.

As her last name started with the letter M, it afforded her much-needed time to learn the 'cookie prayer.' At first, she thought to ask her father, Len, to help her memorize the words, but then decided against it. It was one thing having to attend a Catholic school for its proximity to home, yet quite another thing to admit that she was actually saying one of 'their' prayers. As the days passed by, all she could remember was the opening line, "Our Father who art in Heaven." Her constant worry and anxiety blocked any possibility of remembering any more of the prayer.

On the momentous day of the milk and cookie prayer debut, she still had not memorized the prayer. Instead, Candy decided to put all of her focus on praying for a miracle. Squeezing her eyes tightly shut and trying to will herself to be invisible, she was startled back to reality when she heard her name called. Walking very slowly, she made her way to the front of the class and locked her eyes on the bleeding statue of Jesus hanging on the wall. Trying to steady herself, she held her hands up in prayer position, lowered her head, closed her eyes and said in a tiny, trembling voice, "Our Father who art in Heaven ..." and that's as far as she got.

But it didn't matter, because suddenly the nuns and the other children belted out the rest of the prayer at the top of their voices. Bowing her head even lower, Candy started to move her lips as if she were reciting along with the others. When they finished, she lifted up her head and loudly said, "Amen." The sister who led her back to her seat commented on how reverent she had been by keeping her head bowed the entire time.

Unfortunately, her opportunity to develop her Catholic education would come to an abrupt halt after only eighteen months, as the county decided to build a highway straight through the middle of her family's property. After her parents were compensated with an increase on what they had originally paid for the farm, the family moved to another beautiful property further east on Long Island.

The mere mention of Long Island conjures up gorgeous oceanfront homes in fashionable communities like the Hamptons where celebrities and the rich and famous hang out. Their new house in the sleepy little town of East Moriches was about a thirty-minute drive west of the trendy Hamptons. Unlike its more glamorous neighbors, the East Moriches township had only one school, one traffic light on Main Street, and one Mister Smith who held the most prominence, as he owned the majority of businesses in the town.

The family's new ten-acre home was named *Old Field* and its name was proudly displayed in bold letters on the base of the property's huge flagpole, which had been the towering mast of a ship owned by the property's original occupant, a sea captain.

Their massive, four-story Victorian home overlooking East Moriches Bay held lots of obvious charms along with sixteen-foot ceilings: huge, white wicker swings on the sweeping verandas overlooking the bay and a two-story, stained-glass window adjacent to the winding, mahogany staircase.

Claire's choice of new home made Angel Ariel's heart sing, for it was almost the exact replica of the wonderful ocean-side Victorian that she and her Twin-Flame Kiel shared in Heaven during many a hiatus from their physical incarnations.

The second floor had a sunroom at the front of the house completely surrounded by windows. These ocean-facing rooms were very common in 18th and early 19th century homes along the bay. In anticipation of the return of their husbands, the wives of sea-faring men would gaze out at the horizon for a glimpse of their husbands' returning ships. In fact, the whole area surrounding her new home had quite a sea-faring feel about it. Shortly after the family's move, Candy discovered how fortunate she truly was to have a whole wealth of historical maritime relics right next door.

Mrs. Osborne, the next-door neighbor, was eighty years old and a sea captain's widow. Her solid frame and hearty bosom portrayed a woman of strength and character. The moment Candy walked through her house, she felt like she was stepping onto the deck of a ship. Mementos of Mrs. Osborne's deceased husband's life spent at sea were proudly displayed throughout the house. The ship's clock, its steering wheel and even its nude, busty masthead graced her living room. There were all sorts of interesting souvenirs, including sharks' teeth, old, weathered maps and worn, yellowed photographs of distant exotic ports.

On their many visits, Candy's brothers were in complete awe of Mrs. Osborne's collection. Yet it soon became apparent as to why Candy showed such a keen interest in all things maritime. As far as she was concerned, the greatest contribution that Mrs. Osborne ever made to her life was by being grandmother to two adorable boys, Peter and Paul.

Knowing full well that Mrs. Osborne's grandsons would be visiting, Candy would get dressed in her best outfit, complete with white go-go boots, which were all the rage in the 1960s. She would then nonchalantly go visit Mrs. Osborne and feign surprise as the two boys appeared on the other side of the door. One was a year older than she was and the other a year younger. She drove herself crazy trying to decide which grandson she liked better.

At almost ten years of age, Candy was 'cluey' enough to have seen crucifixes prominently displayed in many of Mrs. Osborne's rooms and she knew that Peter and Paul were not your typical Jewish names. One afternoon while she, Peter and Paul were munching on milk and cookies in Mrs. Osborne's sunny kitchen, Candy sought to impress these handsome lads and told them with great conviction that before moving, she too had also attended a Catholic school. She was sure that this revelation would make them fall madly in love with her. Yet it turned out that they respected her ability to catch frogs and dig for clams much more than her short association with their religion.

Needless to say, Candy couldn't have been happier that her family moved to such a lovely home. But, counter to its outside beauty and charm, this house would soon reveal a dark, hidden secret. Ultimately, this would have a dramatic effect on Candy's connection to all things spiritual.

Like many old houses, this one had its fair share of interesting nooks and crannies and Candy loved exploring this grand old lady. Yet, her perception of her new home would dramatically change the first time she and her older brother set foot in the basement. Descending the dimly lit steps, Candy instantly felt uneasy and she froze. Her heightened intuition picked up the labored breathing of a dark, foreboding presence. Her older brother noticed that she had stopped and told her that there was nothing to worry about. Going against her feelings, Candy forced herself to follow her brother in order to further explore the maze of dank rooms. Suddenly she felt a stifling energy grab her and hold her tightly.

Suffocating and clutching her chest, she ran back up the steps and never went down in the basement again. From then on, even when she merely passed the basement door, her whole body would shudder in terror. Unlike other times, she did not attempt to share her experience with her parents and this time forced herself to forget it ever happened. Although the basement obviously held unwelcome energy, the house came with some wonderful new additions. One of those was a shiny, black Steinway baby grand piano on which Candy took her first piano lessons.

The formal lounge room with its tastefully chosen antiques and high ceilings seemed like a beautiful, elegant backdrop for the study of music, but for one exception. Upon entering the room, Candy's intuitive awareness sensed a dark presence watching her. In fact, she felt the temperature of the room was noticeably colder than the other rooms and when she was playing the piano, she would actually see the icy appearance of her breath before her. Although she felt uneasy, she would continue to practice, as she greatly desired to please her parents. Once again, she told no one about her impressions and kept these feelings of fear locked deep inside.

It was shortly after experiencing the negative energy in the basement and the uneasy feeling in the piano room that Candy started to have recurring nightly visits from a stranger. Her bedroom looked like it was decorated for a princess with a canopy of delicate, white lace covering her white four-poster bed. And while it appeared to be the perfect place for peaceful slumber, she would absolutely dread falling asleep every night.

As she drifted off to sleep, Candy felt the weight of an evil energy that grabbed her. Night after night, she would bury herself under a mountain of stuffed animals, trying desperately to fight off sleep. Yet each time her exhausted body would eventually give in to rest, this vile entity would kidnap her soul. Not having the knowledge of how to spiritually protect herself, all of her attempts to stop his assaults were futile. Frightened by these horrible visits, Candy once again tried to speak up but was told that it was all in her imagination and she buried this episode deep within her and did the unimaginable. She turned off her psychic abilities and stopped all of her angelic connections, closing herself off from anything to do with spirituality.

After being so open to the beautiful angelic realm, she was not at all prepared for the dark, evil side of life. (It would be forty years later that, through spiritual healing and past life regression, Candy learned that this man who kidnapped her at night was a pedophile who had lived and died in this house. Refusing to go to the light to face the life he chose to lead, his soul was trapped on the Earth plane. In his nightly visits to Candy, he would take her soul away to a dilapidated cabin in another dimension to rape her.)

Angel Ariel looked down from Heaven and wept. Using her free will to turn off her angelic connection and psychic gifts would be the most significant event in Claire's entire life. Shutting herself off from her Divine eternal nature, she forgot who she was.

3

Prevention is Better than Cure

Upon getting her family resettled, Candy's mother prepared to welcome some new guests. After investigating goat breeders on Long Island, she bought a very large, odorous male goat along with his three wives who took up residence in the grand old carriage house that had been converted into a barn. Candy's older brother, Sandy, was given the chore of milking and tending the goats. As the billy goat was ornery and rather territorial, Candy was very grateful that this task was not left to her. With the extra room on the property, a hen house was constructed and chickens soon moved in. The job of looking after them and collecting their organic eggs was bestowed upon Candy.

Although her chore seemed to be less dangerous than looking after the goats, it had its challenges as well. She soon learned that some of the chickens were not at all delighted in having their eggs removed. They would often silently wait as she entered the chicken coop and then suddenly fly in her face as they squawked and flapped in defiance. As with most childhood chores, it taught her responsibility, that if she did not feed and water her rather bad-tempered, feathery friends, they would die.

Once Candy's mother discovered that her brother's asthma could be prevented by introducing something as simple and natural as goat's milk, it opened up a whole new world of alternative living. This one event started her family's lifelong quest and devotion to health. As her parents began to acquire all things healthy, the house started to fill up with holistic books, publications and products to help them raise their family in the most natural of ways. One of the many health magazines that her parents subscribed to was called *Prevention*.

This magazine featured various articles and advertisements on the benefits of health products and natural supplements. Candy had no doubt that the seeds of the first organic garden were planted in her mother's mind after she read this health 'bible.' As young children, Candy and her brothers became well versed in Linus Pauling's theory on the health benefits of massive doses of Vitamin C and Adele Davis's tips on organic gardening. By reading the magazine, her parents would educate themselves on the vitamin and mineral supplements that would be the most beneficial. Having completed their research, they would then introduce the latest supplements into their family's diet.

From that moment on, Sylvia was totally devoted when it came to looking after her family's health. In fact, Candy's skin glowed with vitality because her cells were being well nourished. Yet as a young girl, Candy could not have cared less about optimum vitality. As far as she was concerned, if all her friends were eating artificial flavoring, preservatives and artificially colored foods, she wanted to be just like them.

When her mother would offer her the latest health concoction, Candy would turn up her nose and refuse to eat it. Never taking no for an answer, her mother replied, "I'm not doing this for you, I am nourishing the cells of my future grandchildren!"

Once her parents decided that their family would live a healthy lifestyle, there was no holding them back. Healthy living meant that there was to be nothing in the house that contained sugar, artificial flavoring, preservatives, chemicals, additives or coloring. And once the decision had been made, the 'evil' foods were removed in kamikaze fashion. Candy watched in absolute horror as her mother ruthlessly purged the cupboards of all the processed and packaged foods and threw everything into the garbage.

Hours later, feeling very satisfied with all her hard efforts, her mother looked outside the kitchen window to the overflowing trash cans, only to see her young daughter leaning into one of them. Nine-year-old Candy figured that her mother had gone absolutely crazy and this would be the last chance she would ever have to eat ice cream again.

From then on, the family's pantry began to burgeon with whole, nutritious foods and ingredients, and within a short amount of time, it resembled a small health food store. Actually, to be honest, it was better stocked and more comprehensive. The shelves were groaning under the weight of vitamin and mineral supplements of every description. Items like Brewer's yeast, lecithin, wheat germ, desiccated liver powder, apricot kernel oil, shark cartilage, flax seed oil, cod liver oil, vegetable based salts, huge jars of organic honey, unsweetened, carob-coated treats, large vats of stone ground, organic wholemeal flour, organic dried fruits, black strap molasses and many more natural, unprocessed items graced the shelves. The contents defied the imagination.

Looking back, it is a wonder that Sylvia had any time left in the day to sleep. This amazing woman not only managed the property her family lived on and raised four children, but she made her own goat cheese and canned the organic tomatoes from the garden so that her family could have delicious soups in the bitter, cold winter. She vacuum-sealed and canned ripe plums, peaches and apricots for naturally sweetened compotes, while honing her skills and weaving magic to turn the organic, stone ground flour into wonderful breads. Although the bread was healthy, it did have an unfortunate tendency to be very soft and it crumbled easily.

Candy's lunch box would contain organic, unsweetened jam and natural peanut butter sandwiches on crumbly organic bread, along with a glass canning jar of goat's milk. This organic, fully nutritious fare was a fine lunch to eat at home. Yet, once again, Candy would feel the weight of being different whenever she sat down in the school cafeteria and compared her lunch to those of her classmates.

It's true that Candy's little cheeks may have been glowing with health and her cells were completely nourished, but all she wanted was to be like everyone else. And it was the next episode in which she tried to fit in that prompted yet another scolding.

Inviting a new girlfriend to her home after school, eleven-year-old Candy introduced her to her mother. Her new friend excitedly told Sylvia how much she loved her baking. Not having met this girl before, Sylvia was intrigued by the young girl's comment. Candy's face turned white as her friend explained that she often traded her boring white bread for Candy's wonderful, homemade sandwiches.

THWACK!

After her new friend left, while she was being scolded Candy thought that perhaps her mother should have been happy in some small way that she was contributing to the health of this poor 'devitalized,' malnourished girl. Obviously, by the tone and volume of the scolding, her mother did not share her point of view.

As time went by, her parents acquired a great wealth of knowledge about holistic health and they became good soldiers armed with all the weaponry to fight against conventional living. This journey meant that there was an even greater variety of new products that constantly appeared as they were added to the family's daily fare. So it was not at all surprising to see a very large, industrial juicing machine make its appearance, gracing their kitchen counter.

Returning home from school, Candy was greeted by the deafening grinding sounds of the new juicer as her mother processed organic vegetables and fruits. Every afternoon, Sylvia would lovingly prepare a large glass of carrot juice for her family to drink. Although very healthy for her cells, Candy longed for the after-school snacks of milk and cookies that she had seen on television. As carrots were not one of her favourite vegetables, she would hold her nose and gulp it down as fast as she could. With a look of horror, her mother would shout, "Drink it slowly, masticate it, digestion begins in the mouth." She couldn't even postpone the inevitable drinking of the juice by saying, "I'll drink it later," because when the juicing was completed, she had to drink it immediately; otherwise, God forbid, it would oxidize!

As a young child, Candy and her brothers were well versed in the meaning of words like 'devitalized,' 'masticate' and 'oxidize'. It was at this point that Candy should have counted her blessings at having to drink only carrot juice, because not long after that, the 'combinations' began!

It's important to state here that Candy never liked to mix her foods. For example, if given meat, potatoes and peas on the same plate, they must not touch each other, and she would eat them separately. (This was definitely a form of control because she was powerless in so many other areas of her life.) It was for this reason that she was really unhappy when the combinations began. It started off slowly with the introduction of apples to the carrot juice. Then several days later, one could taste the sly introduction of celery to the mix. And then, over time, beetroot and parsley would make their way into the healthy concoction.

Not content with just vegetable and fruit combinations, her mother's creative flair flourished. After reading about the health benefits of a certain item, she started to introduce it into the carrot juice combinations. In time, she honed these concoctions to perfection into something that was lovingly referred to as 'The Drink'.

Although the ingredients of 'The Drink' were never written down, it most often featured a base combination of raw liver, raw eggs, Brewer's yeast, wheat germ, lecithin, raw almonds, apricot kernel oil, black strap molasses and sundry other ingredients that were brimming over with natural goodness. Strange that it was nicknamed 'The Drink' because its consistency was so thick that a spoon could literally stand up in it; there was no way that one could possibly drink it. Yet 'The Drink' did come with one household rule – one could not leave the house in the morning until it was consumed. Subsequently, Candy was always terribly scrawny and didn't want to eat very much of anything at home.

While her mother saw to the care and healthy feeding of her

children, her father was every bit of an enthusiastic advocate of all things natural. He practiced meditation, yoga, deep breathing, and connecting with nature. Unlike his wife who looked after all of the family's needs in the kitchen, her father had the enormous task of putting out the week's vitamins and supplements. His weekly job was to line up the pill vials like little brown soldiers on the pool table and put out a week's worth of supplements for the entire family. Each vial contained about twenty pills including vitamins A, B, C and D, calcium, chromium, zinc, fish liver oil, enzymes, acidophilus, magnesium, selenium, folic acid, iron, etc. etc. Every morning, Candy and her brothers were given their own vial to start the day.

One morning, Candy was sitting in the huge kitchen of the family home. The cold of the Long Island winter found her snuggled next to the open slats of the old-fashioned, freestanding radiator. As the pill vial was presented to her, she felt her throat closing up. Feeling positively ill at the thought of forcing all those pills down her throat, she began to formulate a plan.

Months later, her parents decided to repaint the kitchen. After the painters removed the old radiator to facilitate their job, hundreds and hundreds of pills were found stuffed into the open slats. The solid pills were still intact but the soft vitamin E and fish oil capsules had burst from the heat and melted into a gelatinous mess against the warmth of the radiator.

THWACK!

As her mother was spanking her, Candy was wondering if she was being punished because of all the money that was wasted on the pills or because, somehow, with not taking the pills for so long, her cells and tissues had started to deteriorate. Perhaps her mother was so angry because she would have to start nourishing her daughter all over again.

These formative years between the ages of six and twelve are very important to a child, as they greatly desire to be accepted and to fit in. When Candy closed herself off to her spirituality, she lost her closest friends – her angelic connections – and she felt terribly alone.

Angel Ariel had watched her beautiful student every moment and saw how deeply depressed she had become. Wishing to fill the emptiness in Claire's heart, she sent her a kindred friend in the form of a lovely, wavy-haired girl by the name of Cheryl.

From the moment they met in the third grade, Candy and Cheryl were absolutely inseparable. Candy found it amazing that Cheryl's family was just like the families on television. Her large, boisterous Italian family of uncles, aunties, cousins, nieces and nephews seemed to get together for endless gatherings. Although the reasons for the gatherings changed, there were always people waving their hands in the air, grabbing and kissing one another and speaking at the top of their voices. She was soon treated like Cheryl's adopted little sister as she was welcomed and loved by her family's wonderful cast of characters.

Rarely having contact with her own relatives, Candy lapped up all the attention. Whether these get-togethers were celebrating a birth, communion, birthday, wedding or funeral, the central focus for all these occasions was always on the food. The different locations may have all been in East Moriches, Long Island, but as far as Candy was concerned, she was in Heaven!

The fare at these family gatherings was a cornucopia of all the foods forbidden in Candy's household. Her eyes were as big as saucers as she looked at long tables groaning under the weight of potato chips, pretzels and sodas. Being Jewish, she was presented with a veritable feast of shellfish and pork products, which are strictly prohibited under Jewish law. Like a prisoner who has been denied freedom of choice, she of course ate everything and could not stuff the food into her mouth fast enough.

Cheryl's pantry was always filled to the brim with sugared cereals like Coco Pops, Frosted Flakes, Lucky Charms and the whitest of white breads. Packages of store-bought cookies, candies, chocolate and every kind of soda defied Candy's imagination. If it had sugar, additives, artificial coloring, flavoring or preservatives, it was in there! Opening her friend's pantry was like being in a free supermarket without any parents looking over her shoulder.

In fact, one of Candy's favorite games at Cheryl's house was hide and seek. Cheryl would hide and Candy would go directly to her pantry and start stuffing all the forbidden food into her mouth. Having eaten far too much, she would invariably return home physically ill.

Assessing Candy's upset stomach, her mother would say that her pure body was rejecting the devitalized food that she had eaten. However, holding her swollen stomach and feeling very sick, Candy surmised that it was more the quantity of food she had consumed rather than the quality that had the greatest contribution to her illness.

Unfortunately, Sylvia knew of alternative cures to solve the problem of an upset stomach. The solution was to give her daughter lavender oil to drink. This pungent oil either made one vomit, thus purging the 'demon' food, or it caused one to have diarrhea. Either way, for days after, one would burp up an oil cloud that carried the tell-tale smell as a not-so-subtle reminder of what happens when one veers off the path of health. In the end, no matter how sick Candy would make herself, she decided that the forbidden treats were always worth it.

Cheryl's mom, Mrs. P, was exactly like the mothers on television. Candy always thought it was strange that she should have the same first name as her own mother because, to Candy's young mind, they were so vastly different. Mrs. P was always dressed neat as a pin and kept busy with church and charity organizations. She spent her days baking cakes from magazine recipes, participating in church activities and sewing Cheryl's clothes. Yet the most welcomed difference for Candy was when she was invited to Cheryl's home for a play date.

Arriving at Cheryl's after school was like walking on hallowed ground. Mrs. P always had an afternoon snack tray prepared to greet the girls. Candy marvelled at how they were the exact same snacks that she had seen on television. The forbidden cow's milk came in little wax cartons with straws and the little donuts and cakes were store-bought and wrapped in cellophane. Cheryl and Candy would take their trays and quietly tiptoe into the lounge room. Silently eating their snack, they would sit with Mrs. P as she watched her afternoon soap opera, *The Secret Storm*. And no matter how the episode ended, Mrs. P would always say, "Jeez, I did not see that coming!"

It struck Candy as very odd that this was Mrs. P's afternoon ritual because she hardly ever saw her own mother sit down. Between running the family properties, cleaning, looking after four children, baking bread, canning, tending goats and weeding the huge, organic vegetable garden, there weren't enough hours in the day to eke out any so-called 'quality' time for herself.

Another difference that Candy took particular note of was that Cheryl's family was Catholic. Candy surmised that Mrs. P was quite a strict Catholic, for she not only had crucifixes of Jesus in every room of their house, but she even had a magnetized statuette of Mother Mary on the dashboard of her car. When she would drive to the hairdresser for her weekly comb-out, Cheryl and Candy would sometimes be invited to go along with her. Sitting in the back seat of the lemon yellow Studebaker, Candy's eyes would be transfixed; glued to the face of the disappointed-looking Madonna staring back at her. She was absolutely certain that a good Jewish girl like herself must have been committing a very large sin driving around in a car that was continually being blessed by Mother Mary.

At the beauty salon, the girls would giggle and fool around while Mrs. P was having her hair done. Sometimes when the other hairdressers were not busy, they'd fuss and play with the girls' hair. The best part of their trips was that it was right next door to a diner. Mrs P would give the girls money for what was, in Candy's mind, the holy trinity – hamburgers, French fries and Cokes. And it tasted divine!

After what seemed like an endless summer, the cooler fall air saw the girls starting the fifth grade together. On this particular day, both girls were very excited as they hurried home from school. Kicking the colorful piles of autumn leaves, they clutched a flyer announcing that there would be a Halloween parade and costume contest at the school auditorium, with prizes awarded for the best costumes. The girls had decided that they were going to be fairy princesses with wands and lovely, sheer wings. Racing into Cheryl's home, they excitedly showed the flyer to Mrs. P and asked if she could sew their costumes. With a gentle smile, she said she would love to, and the girls gleefully danced around the room.

Leaving Cheryl's house, Candy ran all the way home. Bursting into the kitchen, she showed her mother the flyer and told her of their plans. Candy's mother briefly glanced up from the pots on the stove and said, "Yes, that sounds nice, dear," although Candy knew that she had not really heard her. To make sure, Candy decided to tell her mother again the following morning. Ignoring her daughter's enthusiasm, Sylvia said that there would be a better chance of winning the first prize if the costumes were original. She decided that Candy and her brothers would go as the Beverly Hillbillies and each child would take a goat with them to the costume parade. Although Candy was heartbroken and desperately wanted to fit in, she had to follow her mother's suggestion.

On Halloween night, Candy's family arrived at the school. One of her brothers was dressed as Jed and the other one was Jethro. Wearing an oversized dress with a scarf tied around her head, Candy was meant to be Granny. All three of the children were pulling reluctant goats into the auditorium. Candy's heart sank as she saw Mrs. P and Cheryl in the audience. Cheryl was wearing a pink, satin fairy costume with transparent wings that her mother had made. She looked so beautiful. Immediately when the school children saw the goats, they started to point and laugh. But the worst part was when the parade started. Dragging the terrified and trembling goats onto the stage literally scared the shit out of them. Between the lights and all the people, they started to relieve themselves all over the stage. This experience, followed by the constant teasing at school, made Candy wish that she could escape her life.

Cheryl's dad worked as a mechanic for an airline. As he was

always fixing machine parts, the grease never totally disappeared from his hands. By contrast, Candy's father, Len, was a lawyer and his uniform was a suit and tie. In later years, Candy always thought how incongruous it was that her father had such a soft, gentle, poet's soul and yet he was a lawyer. Being around Candy's dad was like Disneyland. He would tell jokes and stories, sing songs and recite poems that he wrote for his children. Whatever he touched seemed to have a magical quality.

Her father carefully orchestrated each of Candy's birthday parties to encompass joy and wonderment. Len planned detailed treasure hunts, carefully writing out clues for his daughter and a dozen or more of her giggling friends. He'd give them the first clue and say, "On your marks, get set, go!" Then he'd sit back and watch them try to figure out each clue, which lead to the next clue and then eventually to prizes at the end. He did get himself into a bit of a sticky situation at Candy's twelfth birthday party when he decided to judge a beauty pageant with the girls as contestants. All her friends wiggled and walked the imaginary catwalk and at the end, everyone squealed, "Who won?" Thinking fast on his feet, Len said, "Everyone wins!" upon which he was 'attacked' by a dozen giggling pre-pubescent girls.

One of the fondest memories Candy had of her father was after one of these birthday parties. He piled all her friends into his silver-blue stretch Lincoln with the suicide doors, and took the carload of girls for a ride. This latest Lincoln Continental had a state-of-the-art eight-track tape player and Leonard Bernstein's overture to *Candide* was blaring through the speakers. It was then that her father revealed an amazing feature of this car. Stopped at a traffic light, he pushed a button, and the car full of girls watched in awe as the convertible top folded back into the trunk by itself. (Remember, this was 1967!) There are moments you remember when time seems to stand still; this was one of those times for Candy.

By his own admission, Len called himself either 'good-time Charlie' or 'Peter Pan'. It's not that he didn't take any of the responsibility for raising his children; it's just that he was so good at the fun stuff that Candy's mother was the disciplinarian by default. Because her mother shouldered so much of the burden of child rearing (THWACK!), her father was afforded the time to spend connecting with his children. Candy had so many lovely memoires of her dad, yet there was one in particular that seemed to stand out from the rest, as it demonstrated her father's understanding of his daughter's feelings.

While in the sixth grade, Candy brought a notice home from school about a Parent-Teacher Association's film night about young girls approaching womanhood and menstruation. The film would be shown at the local fire station hall and all mothers and daughters were welcome to attend and bring a baked good to share afterwards. When Len asked Sylvia if she would be taking Candy to the meeting, she replied, "I don't have time for that. For goodness sake, she lives on a farm. All she has to do is look outside and see the goats and dogs doing it." Her father decided to take her to the film presentation himself and was the only father in the hall that night. Candy beamed with pride that her dad had accompanied her.

Driving through the tollbooth at one of the many bridges leading into New York City, Len used to give the tollbooth operator the exact money and flippantly say, "Keep the change." One of Candy's first forays into the world of teenage independence saw her parents actually allow her to go to a local diner with a girlfriend to get hamburgers; their reins on the whole health issue had relaxed quite a bit by then. Both meals together came to $9.95 and Candy gave the waiter a ten-dollar bill. Emulating her father, she said, "Keep the change." The waiter was so incensed that she'd only given him a five-cent tip that he threw it back at her. She couldn't understand his reaction and why he was so upset, as every time her dad had used this same line at the tollbooth everyone had laughed.

Along with his sense of humor, her father also had a healthy wariness for conventional education as he saw its conformity and limitations. He loved travelling and experiencing different people and their varied cultures. When Candy was eight years old, her father told the school principal that he would be taking his children out of school for three months to travel. As he planned to tutor his children while they were away, he asked the teacher to prepare the necessary homework assignments so they would not fall behind in their schoolwork. When the teacher said that she couldn't do that because the children would miss too much, Len calmly replied, "I believe their horizons will be broadened much more by our travels than by sitting in your classroom."

The first of these family trips was to Jamaica. Len had befriended a Jamaican lawyer and Candy's family stayed with his relatives. There always seemed to be people coming and going with a constant stream of friends, uncles, aunties and a rather odd, toothless grandmother who was always cooking.

Standing over a huge stove, Grandma would stir large pots of bubbling liquid as she occasionally added various herbs and spices. The lack of screens on the windows and the open doors enticed all sorts of lizards and other reptiles to live in the house. Once they got a whiff of Grandma's soup, they were hypnotized by the inviting aroma and seemed to drunkenly dance into the kitchen. One day, Candy watched as Grandma prepared a huge pot of soup for dinner. While slowly stirring the pot, she spotted one of these sneaky critters on the wall above the stove. Without missing a beat, she threw her wooden spoon high into the air and knocked him on the head. The blow loosened his grip on the wall and he plummeted face first into the soup. Retrieving her weapon of choice, Grandma looked over at Candy, winked and smiled a wide, toothless grin as she continued to stir the pot. She must have figured a little bit more meat, wherever it came from, could go a long way to feed all the hungry mouths in the household. Candy never mentioned anything to anyone as she thought it must be a local island custom.

The next adventure came one year later when her family spent three months in Acapulco, Mexico. With such a large family to feed, they spent a lot of the time at the local markets. Traipsing in and out of the colorful stalls, Candy and her brothers absorbed all the different sights, smells and tastes of Mexican life. She watched poor peasant men dragging large sacks of oranges down from the mountains to sell at the market. Being one of the most tenacious bargain hunters in the world, her mother was in her absolute element. Large sacks of juicy oranges were only $5, but she insisted on offering these skinny, malnourished mountain men only $2 a bag. In the end, her mother's persistence would wear down their patience and they reluctantly accepted her lower offer. As her mother would triumphantly cart away the huge sacks, Candy's father would linger behind her. He felt so sorry for these impoverished men that he would give them a wink and slip $5 into their hands. This way all parties were happy.

Another two years lapsed and the family found themselves in Puerto Rico. The only thing that twelve-year-old Candy chose to remember from that trip was her penchant for Latino boys with olive skin and large, warm, brown eyes. She daydreamed constantly and would lean out of the window at night watching people dancing in the square and swaying to the rhythms of the loud salsa music that filled the air.

Those years from third to sixth grade contained some of Candy's happiest memories. In addition to having Cheryl as her best friend, she had made many other friends and finally felt like she belonged; she felt normal. At the end of sixth grade, as her primary school graduation drew near, Candy was very excited. Each year, the senior class went on an end-of-year trip to Washington, D.C. All year long, her class had held different bake sales and raffles to save money for the trip. This meant a five-hour Greyhound bus ride with all her friends and a chaperoned stay in a hotel with boys and girls sleeping on separate floors.

As her parents read the informational flyer on the trip, they told Candy that they didn't trust the teachers to look after that many students and announced that she couldn't go. Candy was speechless; she could not believe what she was hearing. Though she pleaded and begged, her words fell on deaf ears. In the end, she was the only child out of her entire class who didn't go on the trip. Broken-hearted that her best friend could not come along, Cheryl sent her a postcard from the nation's capital signed by all her girlfriends. When Cheryl returned, she showed Candy pictures of herself and her friends taken in their hotel room. Dressed in their pajamas, the girls had all crammed onto one bed, laughing and giggling as they waved to the camera. That night, as Candy sat in her bedroom looking down at the snow globe of the Lincoln Memorial that Cheryl had bought her, large tears dropped onto the joyous photos of her friends. It was then that Candy wished that she were dead.

Although she had tried many times to communicate what would have brought her joy, her needs and desires were not acknowledged as being of any importance. Trying to speak up seemed useless and she decided that she was not worth listening to. As she spiralled into a world of silencing her desires, her accumulated sadness had a devastating effect on her physical health. The body can only be sad for so long, before it sends a wake -up call in the form of illness. It was at that point in her life that she began to develop breathing problems.

The day after the class had returned from Washington, the children were all abuzz with their adventures about their trip. Her classmates' excitement wore heavy on Candy's heart and made her feel as if she was suffocating. She was very happy when the school bell finally signalled the end of the day and she began to walk home. Yet she didn't get past the school gates before she suddenly collapsed and felt a constrictive pressure in her chest. Quite simply, she couldn't breathe. Seemingly out of nowhere, she had all the symptoms of a full-blown asthma attack.

She would lie in bed, wheezing as she tried to force air into her constricted lungs. This debilitating condition would last for days as she hung her head over steaming pots of water to try to open up her lungs. The accumulated years of feeling different and not being acknowledged finally caused her system to shut down. This suffocating illness was a direct reflection of the suffocation she felt in her life.

It was in her twelfth year that her family's life would take yet another turn. Through his law practice, Candy's father had gained a new client who described his beautiful farm property in Virginia where his wife and children lived. He explained that he commuted to New York for work, spending four days up north and three days with his family each week. The more he described the lush, green, rolling hills filled with cows and horses and the beautiful lifestyle his family enjoyed, the more the seeds were planted in Len's mind to uproot the family and move to Charlottesville, Virginia.

At her primary school graduation, her girlfriends were happily talking about what it would be like to start Centre Moriches Junior High School together the following year. Candy was heartbroken to be leaving Cheryl and her friends. Having put all her strength and emotional energy into finally fitting in, she now felt like her heart was being ripped out.

The last time she went to Cheryl's house, Mrs. P had made a goodbye dinner in her honor. The table was set with sunny, bright yellow paper plates and balloons. She hugged Candy tightly and gave her a card with a beautiful, smiling sun on it that read, *'We will sure miss your sunny smile around here.'* Candy kept that card for years until it yellowed and fell apart. Every time she read it, she remembered how special Mrs. P had made her feel.

Angel Ariel watched Claire's heart break as she said goodbye to her cherished friend. Wiping the tears from her own eyes, Angel Ariel knew that we learn our best lessons through challenging times, and that Claire was about to get another chance for huge personal growth.

4

A Second Visit Home

Moving to Charlottesville, Virginia, meant getting used to being the new kid again. Candy's parents enrolled her in an A-list, prestigious educational institution called Belfield School. No ordinary school, Belfield was an Ivy League preparatory school for the offspring of the wealthy. The children were chauffeur-driven by the black help in jeeps that proudly displayed the name of their family's property on the side of the vehicle. These children came from very famous bloodlines and they took every opportunity to tell you whom they were. One of Candy's classmates was the grandson of the Kellogg's cereal empire.

These fledgling socialites in training had been brought up with wealth and breeding and carried an air of privilege and social prestige because of their famous heritage. Candy felt inferior and tried to be as invisible as possible.

Seeing how terribly low and alone Claire was, Angel Ariel once again sent her a lovely new friend to help her smile.

Immediately upon their meeting in the seventh grade, Candy and Andrea were drawn to one another. Tall, thin and blonde, Andrea's freshly scrubbed, dewy complexion was what some people called 'peaches and cream'. When she gracefully walked by, one caught the delicate scent of fine-milled, perfumed soap. While her last name didn't mean much to Candy at the time, her family came from extreme wealth and she wore it like a second skin. Walking into their exquisite home on the grounds of Farmington Country Club, Candy felt like she had stepped into a *Town & Country* magazine. The maid, dressed in the traditional grey and white pinafore uniform, met her at the door and took her coat. Andrea seemed to float down the winding staircase as she came to greet her. Unlike the other children in the class, Andrea somehow seemed so untouched by the burden of appearances, as she was very real and down-to-earth.

Over time, their friendship blossomed and they became quite close. But this association was doomed from the start for, even though she and Andrea liked each other very much, when Andrea's parents found out that Candy was Jewish, they forbade her from having Candy as her friend. (One of the stipulations of the country club community was that Jews could not be members.) Hiding the reason from her until many years later, Candy's parents fabricated an explanation. No matter what the reason, she was crestfallen and terribly hurt once again.

With their upcoming graduation from junior high school, her eighth grade class would be treated to a weekend in the moneyed Tides Inn area of Chesapeake Bay. The wealthy parents of one of her classmates owned an enormous home on the water. This mansion had many bedrooms and could easily accommodate the entire class. The weekend's activities included biking, sunning, swimming and boating along the beautiful bay. The permission slip said that boys and girls would be sleeping in separate bedrooms and that several teachers and parents would be supervising.

Again, Candy's parents decided that it was too risky with boys and girls in the same house, so they came up with an alternative plan. It was decided that Candy's family would all go and stay in a nearby motel. This way, Candy could participate in all the activities, but just not sleep over. Crushed once again as she was not being allowed to be a part of her class, and knowing that this was her only alternative, she agreed to it. The only problem was that her younger brothers insisted on hanging around and dampening whatever independent fun she would have had with her friends. This restriction felt like suffocation and her asthma attacks became worse and more frequent.

Having graduated from the exclusive Belfield School, her parents had to decide where she would complete high school. Most of the girls who attended Belfield would continue on to the equally exclusive all girls' high school of St. Anne's. And while Candy interviewed there, her parents ultimately felt that she needed to get a broader experience of life. That fall, at the age of thirteen, she entered Jack Jouette Junior High School.

Immediately upon starting public school, she began to feel a sense of freedom. Without the continual suffocation of 'doing things the correct way' and living up to one's heritage, there seemed to be more of an emphasis on the individual's creative expression. She also loved that she no longer had to wear the navy school blazer with the school's crest, the ridiculous argyle socks and the itchy wool skirts. After two years at Belfield with its manicured lawns and manners, Candy loved expressing herself not only through her choice of school attire, but also in her growing love for creative writing. Expressing herself through poems and stories gave her stifled, stunted voice an outlet. And while she did not dare share her honest writings with her family, she felt better having written down her heartfelt desires and feelings. Not wishing for her work to be discovered, she hid it in a box in the attic next to her room.

Her writing and creative expression gave her so much joy that she joined the school newspaper and the drama club. As she started to enjoy herself, she began to make new friends and loved being a part of these clubs.

It was during that year at junior high that Candy's mother received devastating news. On a routine check-up, Sylvia's doctor discovered a lump in her breast. The doctor told her that it needed to be biopsied straight away to determine if it was benign or malignant. Having spent the last five years shunning conventional medicine and following an organic and alternative lifestyle, Sylvia decided not to have the biopsy and to treat the lump holistically instead.

In her research about health, she had read that Laetrile – also known as amygdaline or Vitamin B17 therapy – was one of the best-known alternative cancer treatments. It works by targeting and killing cancer cells and building the immune system to fend off future outbreaks of cancer. If used in high doses and the Laetrile is of high quality, it is very effective when combined with a strict cancer diet and key supplements. Unfortunately, even though Laetrile is natural and perfectly safe, the U.S. Food and Drug Administration decided to make its purchase illegal and almost impossible to obtain. If doctors used it, they must confess to the FDA that they used Laetrile in their practice, admit to breaking the law and risk having their medical license revoked.

Knowing that there were clinics in Mexico where Laetrile was legal and freely administered, Candy's mother booked into a clinic. This is how, at the young age of thirteen, the mantle of looking after her younger brothers fell to Candy. Each morning, she would set her alarm two hours earlier than her usual wake up time, make breakfast, prepare her own as well as her brothers' school lunches, and make sure that their books and homework were packed. The last thing that she did was to prepare a cup of coffee, take it to her father and wake him up to drive them all to school.

At the end of the day, she would attend to her brothers' homework, prepare dinner for them all, and put them to bed. Afterwards, she cleaned and did the laundry and prepared to do it all again the next day. There was no word as to how long her mother would need to stay for treatments. Candy had to leave her school clubs that gave her much joy, as her sense of duty and responsibility ran very deep.

After three months, Sylvia returned home, completely cancer free. When she paid another visit to her U.S. doctor, he was angry that she had not come in immediately for a biopsy after finding the lump. Taking an X-ray, the doctor was amazed to see that the lump was completely gone. It was then that Sylvia told him about her trip to the Mexican clinic for Laetrile treatments. All the doctor said was that the treatments had nothing to do with the disappearance of the lump, as it was simply a case of spontaneous remission. (Sylvia is alive and well, and cancer-free, to this day.)

For the previous three months, Candy did not know if her mother was going to live or die, yet even with the good news of her mother's healthy return, Candy could not lift her own spirits. Her sadness and loss of hope turned to bouts of depression and she thought a great deal about ending her life.

The constant heaviness on her heart and her feelings of despair, cut through Angel Ariel as she looked on from across the veil. Being unable to interfere with free will, she watched her young charge drowning in a sea of sadness. Angel Ariel shuddered as she realized that her thoughts were foreshadowing the unconscious wish and desire that Claire was formulating in her heart. It was then that Angel Ariel knew that she was not thinking about how to end her life, but that she had asked God to help her exit her physical life early.

As a Spiritual Master Teacher, Angel Ariel knew full well that we all choose in our contract when we will exit our physical, human incarnation. She often laughed when she heard people on the Earth plane say that a certain person had died too soon and should have lived longer. For she knew that we all give ourselves just the right amount of time to learn our contracted lessons and when that time was over, so was our physical existence. But, Angel Ariel also knew that there was a HUGE exception to this rule.

If a soul was experiencing prolonged suffering and deep emotional pain, there were alternative exit points built into their contracts if they really could not endure a human life any longer. She knew that very young souls often did not make it through a whole life, as they had no idea how difficult it is to be human. The only help that Angel Ariel could give was to send her love, for her thoughts of encouragement, reassurance and motivation could no longer penetrate the dense fog of despair that surrounded the teenager.

Trying to escape from a life of not being heard or considered, Candy spent endless hours practicing her beloved piano. By the age of fourteen, her deep love for the instrument was evident in her accomplished playing and was noticed by her parents. One day, after a lengthy time practicing, Candy passed by her parents' bedroom door and overheard their conversation. Sylvia said, "Have you noticed, Candy has become very good at the piano. I was thinking that perhaps we should send her to the School of Performing Arts in New York."

Len's voice quickly countered, "What? Do you want to go and waste your money? She is so pretty. She's just going to marry someone rich and have children and raise a family. Remember, we have three sons who will all need to go to college."

Biting her lip so hard it bled, Candy cried to think that she was not worth the investment. Not having her talents considered worthy of recognition, she put all her efforts into her physical appearance. It was during her teen years that her control issues with food started and her anorexia began.

During the summer of her fifteenth year, Candy's family decided to escape the heat and humidity of Virginia, and rented a home on the beautiful stretch of beach that is Montauk, Long Island. Her parents had allowed her to invite her childhood friend, Cheryl, for the summer. Along with her two younger brothers and their nanny, the family settled in for a relaxing time. They usually spent their days at the Montauk Golf and Racquet Club or sunning and swimming at the beach.

Candy and Cheryl awoke one gloomy morning to the sound of thunder and rain against the window in their bedroom. Her parents came into the room and announced that they had been invited to a luncheon at the club and that, since the weather was inclement, the beach was off limits for the whole day. The girls waited for Candy's parents to leave for their lunch and, as soon as they were gone, grabbed their towels and headed for the ocean.

Running far down the beach, the two friends lay on the sand and watched the effects that the storm was having on the sea. The water was foamy and, although the sea was rough, the weather was still quite warm. Braving the stormy conditions, Candy and Cheryl decided to go for a swim and waded far from the shore. As they happily splashed around, they did not pay attention to the growing swell. They say that you should never turn your back on the ocean and that is exactly what Candy did. In that one moment that she wasn't looking, a huge wave crested behind, sweeping her off her feet, crashing down and crushing her body into the sandy bottom of the sea.

Losing consciousness, Claire immediately heard a whirring sound, like hundreds of bees were trapped in her head. Rising above her body she looked down and gazed at her ragdoll-like form being tossed in the foamy surf. At that moment, she felt a familiar tug as she was sucked into a dark tunnel with a brilliant white light at the end. All of a sudden, a hidden force picked her up and gently propelled her towards the light. As she drew closer to it, she was able to discern a tall being standing at the end of the tunnel. As she came fully into the light, she saw an Angel waiting for her.

Claire felt blissfully peaceful and calm, as she fully remembered that she had had a similar experience when she hit her head in her school playground. The Angel appeared as a tall shard of light and it bent down and touched its head to Claire's forehead. The Angel conveyed telepathically that her prayers had been answered and it lovingly took her hand.

A beautiful garden appeared in front of her, filled with the most wonderful, huge pink roses, and their beautiful scent filled the air. Claire was amazed to see her grandparents who had died smiling and laughing as they waited for her in the garden. Seeing Claire again, their faces lit up with joy and their bodies were very much alive and vibrant. The Angel explained to Claire that many souls who cross over from physical form back to their one true home in Spirit, get to experience a 'welcome home' party with their loved ones. This reunion helps them to recall that, just because they no longer have their physical form, they still exist. The Angel laughed and said that

God knows that whenever we go to an unfamiliar place, we feel much better if we already know people there. Claire delighted in not only seeing her grandparents again, but also her beloved pets that had crossed over as well. Her heart leapt with joy as she was reunited with them.

The Angel conveyed to Claire that it was important to continue her journey to visit the Hall of Justice. Sensing her sadness at leaving her loved ones, the Angel explained to Claire that she could be together with them whenever she desired, as they were only a thought away. Holding hands, Claire and her Angel wended their way to the edge of the beautiful rose garden and came upon a forest. The thick trees made it difficult to see, but the Angel guided their way through the dark woods. Suddenly they broke through and the ground fell away before them. Claire gasped as a vast City of Light appeared before her eyes. Stretching as far as the eye could see in all directions, this city was filled with crystal castles and their spiralling turrets rose high into the air. Claire started to weep as she felt the energies of love, peace and unity coming from the souls living in this magnificent city. A soft breeze carried the faint sound of a sweet angel's choir off in the distance.

The Angel interrupted Claire's reverie, announcing that they must continue to the next part of her journey. Instantly, Claire found herself standing before a large, columned, Greek building. The Angel conveyed that this was the Hall of Justice where everyone goes to review their human incarnation. She accompanied Claire up the marble steps and once at the top, reminded her that everyone must go in and review alone.

Walking into the massive hall, Claire was surprised to see that there was no one else inside and only a single bench. Upon sitting down, she watched holographs of her life appear from birth to the time she drowned. As she watched these images of all her actions, thoughts, words and feelings that she had chosen, she felt exactly what others had felt as a result of those decisions. She smiled as she watched instances in which she was caring, loving and kind, but grimaced as she watched other times when she had lied, was critical or judgmental.

After watching her whole life thus far, Claire sat in silence, reflecting on what she had viewed. The Angel, who had been waiting patiently outside, entered and sat down next to her. Hearing Claire's thoughts, the Angel explained that this review happens for all souls because we are all One and what we do to one person we ultimately end up doing to ourselves. In this way, everyone gets to see what they have caused to happen as the result of the thoughts, words and actions they choose in their lives. So goes the expression, 'What ye shall sow, so shall ye reap'. The Angel added that this is one of the great spiritual laws and no amount of running, hiding or denying that these laws exist will make them not be so.

Taking Claire's hand once more, the Angel explained that it was time to go to the Hall of Akashic Records. At the utterance of the hall's name, another large Greek-looking building appeared. Advancing up the huge marble steps, Claire walked into another grand hall and stood before a group known as the Etheric Council; a group of Ascended Masters and wise, ancient beings that help souls review the contract of their physical incarnation. Sitting in a semi-circle before her, they opened up her contract in her Book of Life and began to discuss the lessons that she had contracted and chosen to learn.

The Council showed Claire that, as a result of not speaking up for herself and asserting her independence, her life became very difficult and she was continually giving away her power. Listening intently to the Elders, Claire was able to clearly see that her great sadness was directly attributed to not being her authentic self.

At the end of reviewing her contract, the Etheric Council then said, "So, are you now choosing to return to complete your contract on Earth?" Startled by their question, in that moment she realized that, unlike the first time she died at the age of five, she now had a choice as to whether or not she would return. With a huge smile on her face, Claire beamed and said, "No, I won't be returning. I have had enough of physical incarnations forever, thank you." Taken aback by her response, the Etheric Council replied, "Hang on, not so fast. Let's take a look at what you will be missing out on."

To entice her to go back and complete her contract, they pointed out that there was to be a marriage in her early twenties. Briefly glancing at the words that she had previously written, Claire looked quite disinterested and told the Council that she did not care. Putting their heads together, they said, "But look here, you are going to be a mother. There are two beautiful children that you will be giving birth to." Once again, totally unfazed, Claire sighed, "I don't care, I am not going back." A long silence followed as the Etheric Council knew that Claire had free will to choose not to return. Slowly, they said, "You know, if you do not go back, your death will devastate your parents and they will never get over it." Suddenly Claire's face dropped, as she had not considered the effect that her death would have on them. It was then that she reluctantly picked up her pen and co-signed with the Etheric Council to return to her Earthly incarnation and fulfill her contract.

Immediately upon signing, Candy rose to the surface of the ocean and began to cough up a great deal of seawater. That night, tucked up in the warmth and comfort of her bed, she remembered the journey that the Angel had taken her on and vowed that she would live her life differently and speak up for herself. But in order to tell her parents of her experience, she would have to divulge that she had disobeyed their orders and had gone to the beach. And even if she did not get into trouble for her disobedience, the sharing of her journey with her Angel would most probably be met with the same disbelief as every other time she had tried to speak of her experiences.

Angel Ariel looked down from Heaven and tried to encourage Claire to speak up for herself. She knew that that was the exact reason that she had unconsciously planned for the wake-up call of her near-death experience. Tuning into Claire's scared energies, Angel Ariel felt her student's courage receding and, just as she expected, Claire chose to silence her voice and bury her experience deep inside; she never spoke of it.

After her second near-death experience, Candy's revisit to her one true home made it very difficult to be back in physical incarnation once more. Her inability to be grounded caused her to be silent and introverted, and she escaped even more into her piano playing.

Seeing Claire withdraw more and more from life, Angel Ariel began to rack her brain as to how she could help her beautiful friend enjoy her physical life. With a flash of inspiration, she decided that it was time to send Claire her first love. Smiling to herself, Angel Ariel sighed as she remembered her first encounter with her beloved Kiel. Being with her Twin-Flame made her feel completely loved and accepted for who she was. Feeling very proud of her wonderful idea, Angel Ariel was suddenly perplexed and said aloud, "But whom will I choose?" In many instances, the choice of a love would be selected from a cherished soul from a former, shared incarnation on Earth. This thought was no help to Angel Ariel as Claire was experiencing her first human incarnation.

She thought back to Claire's attendance in her classroom and remembered a very sweet soul who had just returned from his first incarnation. She recalled how their personalities were so well suited, as they were both quiet dreamers. Looking into his Book of Life, Angel Ariel saw that not only had he decided to return to Earth for another incarnation the same year as Claire, but that they were also living in the same town and going to the same high school. Suddenly, she sensed a flurry of shivers and tingles as confirmation to create a place and time for them to meet.

In the fall of September 1971, two months before her sixteenth birthday, Candy began her tenth grade sophomore year at Albemarle High School. The unusually warm days created by an Indian summer saw the bright sunlight stretch long shadows across the ground until early evening. Having to rely upon her older brother, Sandy, for a ride home, Candy waited patiently after school. Deep in thought about her homework assignments, she was startled when he and his friend snuck up from behind and scared her. Sandy told her that he and a few guys had arranged a touch football match and that he would only be about an hour. Disappointed that she would not be going straight home, the three of them walked over to the football field and Candy sat on the bleachers.

Opening her books, she put her head down and began to read. A loud cheer from the field caught her attention as the rowdy group of boys chose sides. Scanning the players, she recognized many familiar faces, but there were a couple of boys whom she had not seen before. Putting her fingers in her ears, she sought to drown out their shouts and calling of the plays.

After the game was over, her brother signalled that they would be heading home. As she was walking to the car, his friend approached and by his side was one of the sweetest faces she had ever seen. As Stephen was introduced to her, Candy was mesmerized and could not take her eyes off his face. There was something so familiar about him, and she thought for sure that she recognized him, although she could not remember from where. As they chatted, it seemed like they were old friends catching up once more. Suddenly, Sandy burst in and interrupted their conversation, announcing that they needed to be getting home. Stephen tentatively asked if he could call her, and Candy handed him her phone number. Walking her to the car, he opened the door for her, and when they smiled at each other, time stood still.

Watching from Heaven, Angel Ariel danced around in a circle and said, "YES! YES! YES!"

Stephen and Candy were soon inseparable and their quiet, dreamy natures suited each other perfectly. This lovely, tall, lanky German boy with a mop of tight, Adonis curls came from a modest home. Being very soft-spoken, he was painfully shy with adults and he hardly spoke around Candy's parents. His silent and soft demeanor prompted her mother to nickname him 'Harpo', a name that Candy loathed. But he was anything but silent around her, and their kindred friendship grew quickly.

The bond that they shared was of another world and they both sensed that they were very different from typical teenagers. Shunning the usual rebellion and hell raising of their peers, they opted for just spending time together in nature. They loved to hike along the beautiful trails of Skyline Drive overlooking the Blue Ridge Mountains. It was in this relationship that Candy felt her most honest and open, as Stephen listened attentively to her every word, considered her desires and loved her solely for who she was.

As they both entered their senior year of high school, they discussed which colleges they could attend so that they would remain close to one another. But with all their planning, Candy did not realize that her life would, once again, take an extraordinary twist. Returning home from school one day, her parents announced that the family would be moving to Australia. "Where?" replied Candy. Along with the question of "Where?" she should have also been asking the all-important question of "Why?"

Perhaps the answer to this question could be discovered within her father's dream of owning oceanfront property. This life-long desire to own vast stretches of land may have stemmed from his experiences as a child of the Depression. Growing up in the South Bronx in the 1930s, his cramped city conditions afforded him a view of poverty all around him. He described how he had shared a one-bedroom apartment with his parents and older sister, and had slept in a fold-up cot until he was thirteen years old. His inner city experiences must have ignited a longing for a life abounding with space and the beauty of nature. As oceanfront land was prohibitively expensive in the United States, synchronicity stepped in and brought him magical connections that lead him to fulfill his dream of investing in Australia in the 1960s.

At that time there were no celebrities like Steve Irwin, 'The Crocodile Hunter', or movie stars like Hugh Jackman extolling the beauty of the land Down Under. In later years, Candy suspected that, with America's ongoing involvement in the Vietnam War, the fact that her parents had three teenage sons may have been a huge incentive for the family to move overseas. In the end, the reasons for the move did not matter to her breaking heart. All she cared about was that she was being ripped away from the one person who had loved and honored her in every way.

5

Life in a Foreign Land

Candy never did find out the definitive reason as to why they moved, but in July 1973, her family landed in Perth, Western Australia. At seventeen years of age, Candy was once again heartbroken. In the last few months before she left, Stephen and Candy desperately clung to each other and faithfully promised that they would write. He swore that he would work several jobs and save up enough money to come and be with her.

Settling into life in a foreign land, Candy anxiously awaited letters from her boyfriend. As days turned into months, her heart ached terribly as she could not understand why she never received any word from her cherished Stephen. How could he so easily forget her? It was years later that her brother admitted that he and their mother had thrown out all of Stephen's letters when they arrived. Unfortunately, he was not Jewish and as such, she would not have been allowed to marry him. As time went on and Candy didn't hear anything from him, he slipped further and further from her heart.

Along with acclimating to her new life in Australia, Candy got her first taste of what it was like to live in a Jewish community. Being new arrivals, there suddenly seemed to be a lot of people who made it their business to know every facet of her family's life. This is certainly not endemic only to Jewish communities, as the confined parameters of many ethnic cultures often contribute to narrowed perceptions. And without a broader view of humanity, the primary focus and pastime seemed to be spreading gossip. The community members certainly lived their lives always nit-picking and judging others.

Not long after she arrived, Candy was invited to spend the afternoon with a lovely Jewish girl who she met through her brother. When she told her new friend that there seemed to be lots of people interested in her family, she was warned that the entire community made it their business to know everyone else's business. She said, "God forbid that we have bacon one morning and the neighbours smell it! We would read all about it in the local Jewish newspaper the very next day." Candy laughed but her new friend said that she was serious. She added that, if someone chose to keep their life private and didn't provide any interesting tidbits for people to talk about, stories would simply be fabricated about them.

To try to soften the heartbreak of missing Stephen, Sandy wasted no time in introducing his sister to a string of his friends who were also eligible, Jewish pre-med students. The sunny beaches of Perth provided days full of warmth and swimming and she spent the star-filled nights being wined and dined by some of Western Australia's future generations of brilliant doctors and surgeons.

On one sunny weekend, one of those future doctors, (let's call him M), invited Candy to Scarborough Beach; a magnificent stretch of pristine white sand and turquoise water. Yet the breathtaking view of Mother Nature was a distant second to the white bathing suit she had chosen to wear. Unbeknownst to her, the suit became quite transparent when wet.

As she walked along hand-in-hand with M, they approached two friends of his who were lying on the sand. M introduced Candy as his new friend in a somewhat boastful manner, and she felt an urge to take a photo of his friends. Taking her camera from her beach bag, she snapped the first photo of her future husband. And little did she realize the time was drawing near for the birth of the next phase of her life.

By the time she started college in March of 1974, Candy had pretty much acclimated to her new surroundings. The adjustment to life in Australia was probably easier than it would have been in many other countries because the language was the same; or at least it *seemed* to be English. She had experienced a particularly embarrassing episode during a lecture when the young man seated next to her asked her if she had a rubber he could borrow. Terribly embarrassed, she said, "I beg your pardon?"

He repeated the question.

She said, "How dare you ask me such a question?" Her American translation of the word was somewhat different from the Australian version, as her understanding was that 'rubber' was the slang term for condoms. But all this young man wanted was to borrow an eraser.

Candy loved college and soon made many friends. She was a very busy girl juggling assignments and boys. It seemed like the very thing that was not sanctioned by her parents was presented to her in droves; as she had many non-Jewish gentlemen wanting to improve American-Australian relations. At lunch times, she would meet three friends in the school's music room to play piano and jam together. They sounded pretty good and other students hung around and listened to their music. Their sound was noticed by one of the teachers, who asked if they would play at the upcoming sports camp. This three-day event was a great way to introduce the games and sports of the primary curriculum that many of the students would have to teach once they became schoolteachers.

Candy excitedly told her parents that she would be going to this camp and proudly added that she and her group of musicians had been asked to entertain. When she asked her parents for a cheque to pay for the weekend, they said that she couldn't go because there would be boys and girls sleeping at the same camp. Being over eighteen years of age, Candy could not believe what she was hearing and pleaded with them, saying that she must attend as she was playing piano in the camp's talent presentation. Her parents' compromise was that they would provide the funds for her to go as long as she did not sleep over. Once again, Candy was the only one unable to stay over for the whole weekend.

Seeing this repeated scenario, Angel Ariel looked on helplessly as time and time again Claire would fail to assert herself and demonstrate how important it was to have her desires honoured. As Claire finished performing with her band at the camp, Angel Ariel felt the heaviness in her young friend's heart as she left her celebrating classmates and was the only one who had to drive an hour home. Angel Ariel knew that, with Claire's inability to speak up, she continued to allow herself to be controlled. With this realization, Angel Ariel shuddered as she fully knew that whatever manifests in our outer world is a direct reflection of our inner world. By disempowering herself, it was just a matter of time before she drew the same lesson to herself again. But this time, the contrast would be even greater in order to really get her attention. It was not surprising to Angel Ariel when Claire drew one of her most important, controlling teachers to herself.

Her future husband was the apple of his father's eye. His father had lost both his parents in a car accident and had never been able to realize his dream of going on to higher education and becoming a doctor. At the young age of seventeen, he had to provide financially for his younger brothers and sisters.

Never having been able to attend university, he lived vicariously through the academic accomplishments of his youngest child. Going to law school and excelling in public speaking and debating made her future husband quite the 'prince apparent' but for one exception; he had a penchant for dating non-Jewish girls. In his father's eyes, this was reason enough for him to be written out of the will and he had proven the seriousness of this issue by cutting off any communications with other family members who had chosen to marry outside of the faith.

Shortly after being told in no uncertain terms that he should stop dating non-Jewish girls, he found himself sitting in the law school library lamenting his situation with a friend. Their topic of discussion was his disappointment concerning the lack of new, eligible Jewish girls in Perth; as he professed that he had 'gone through' all of them.

Mentioning that there was a new, American Jewish girl in town, his friend was quick to point out that this new girl would not be interested in dating him because she only dated Jewish doctors. Well, that's how it appeared because Candy had dated only her brother's pre-med classmates. To which he arrogantly replied, "She'll go out with me because everyone knows who I am." And, in fact, this was very true in Perth's Jewish community; he was the youngest son of a very wealthy businessman who had made millions from his scrap metal business.

His friend replied, "No, she won't."

To which he quickly retorted, "I'll bet you ten dollars she'll go out with me."

The following week, Candy received his phone call. In a business-like manner, he stated his full name and added, "You know who I am, don't you?"

Candy registered the arrogance in his voice. "Oh yes," she replied in an off-hand manner, "I remember, you're that boy from the beach." She surprised herself by her surly response and wondered why she was acting this way. Not taking any notice, he asked if she would like to go out with him on Saturday night. As Candy already had a date, she said that she wasn't available and quickly added that she would pencil him in for the following Saturday.

As she hung up the phone, Candy wondered if she had chosen the term 'pencil him in' because their date could be so easily erased – perhaps in response to his cocky, egotistical manner. Looking back on their first date together, it seemed that everything on the night was ill fated. If ever Spirit and the Angelic world gave someone warning signs that something was blocked and not free-flowing, their date would prove to be the best example ever.

On that evening of May 4, 1974, Candy stood on the balcony of her family's home watching for the lights of his flashy sports car to crest the top of the hill. She looked down at her dress and was very pleased with herself. The black velvet gown was delicately designed with the faint pattern of Victorian children at play. As it was winter, she had borrowed her mother's suede coat with a huge fox collar and its matching fox hat. Her hands were buried deep in a black fur muff and she looked like something out of a tragic Russian novel.

Upon his arrival, Candy introduced him to her parents. What started out as a polite introduction turned into a lengthy conversation, which delayed the start of their evening. Having made dinner reservations, he explained that they must go, and they hurried off. His attempt to race to the restaurant was greatly hindered because he wasn't quite sure of the address. What should have been a ten-minute drive turned into half an hour. Arriving at a beautiful French restaurant along the waterfront, he quickly ordered for both of them, and announced to the waiter that he had tickets to the theatre and that the play started at eight o'clock. Candy thought how very presumptuous that he hadn't asked his date what kind of food she liked nor whether she had any interest in watching the play that he had booked. His inability to consider anyone else's desires or feelings would continue throughout their marriage.

During dinner, she listened to her date speak at length about his law studies, his debating and his awards. As he extolled his virtues, he fingered his 24-carat gold, monogrammed cigarette lighter next to the gold cigarette case and the tiny mother-of-pearl saccharin holder that he used. Maybe she was a bit naïve and not terribly worldly, but what came to mind were the words 'pretentious' and 'self-important'. Rushing through dinner, they hurried to the playhouse and arrived with minutes to spare.

Just before the lights dimmed and the curtain rose, he noticed one of his lecturers was reading a newspaper in the front row. The play was so awful that when the lights came up during intermission, his lecturer was still reading the newspaper. The play didn't get any better in the second half. Finishing around 10 p.m., they decided to rescue the night by going to Miss Maude's Coffee House, which was one of the only places in Perth that was still open that late in the evening.

Miss Maude's was the most enjoyable part of the whole evening and they chatted quite a long time. Walking back to the parking garage after midnight, they noticed that it was closed for the night and the gate was locked. He was devastated that he could not get his precious sports car out, and all Candy could do was laugh. Walking to the public phones, he woke up his mother and told her of the situation. Taking a taxi to his house, he borrowed his mother's car and drove Candy home.

Looking back many years later, Candy could clearly see why his car had to have been locked up on the night of their first date. It may have been one of the few times that she ever saw him vulnerable. He was helpless to do anything and had completely let his guard down. By exposing his softness, it made him real and it revealed humanity underneath the veneer of his egotistical, moneyed exterior. Unfortunately, he would rarely show this softer side of himself in their many years of marriage.

The day after their first date, a beautiful, gold-monogrammed, pale grey envelope arrived, along with a dozen long-stemmed red roses. The message on the card read, *'Phew, I got my car back!'* It was obvious what his priorities were.

During that year, Candy still dated other men because this new relationship did not become serious until their second year of dating. Well, it was serious for her, as she was now seeing him exclusively and planning her life around his schedule. He, on the other hand, was very much consumed with law school and debating and his ego was constantly stroked by winning many awards. She dutifully followed along to his debate nights and would sit in the audience and watch him perform. After a lifetime of having her desires and wishes silenced, she made his activities and pursuits her priority.

It was in their third year of dating that they had heard that very close friends of theirs, who had only been dating for six months, had decided to get married. On hearing the news of their engagement, Candy was crestfallen and could not hide the shock on her face, as she had now been dating her boyfriend exclusively for three years. Her friends were so concerned about Candy's reaction that they actually came to visit her later that evening and told her not to despair because they were sure that he loved her and would soon get around to asking her to marry him.

Shortly after their friend's wedding, Candy found herself riding in the back seat of his parents' car. Trying to keep her voice to a whisper, she was saying how happy their friends were since their wedding. Disinterested and aloof, he stared out the window and all but ignored her. Getting angrier, Candy finally said, "When two people know each other for three years, something usually happens."

He nonchalantly looked over at her and replied, "Are you asking me to marry you?"

She then foolishly said, "Yes."

In a rather off-the-cuff and detached manner, he simply replied, "OK."

(For the next twenty years of marriage, Candy repeatedly asked her husband to surprise her and propose to her in a beautiful setting, to which he replied, "No, you are a pushy American bitch and you blew your chance by asking me first and not waiting.")

They wed on December 11, 1977, and in true Jewish tradition, there were three hundred and fifty guests at the wedding. Of that huge number, Candy had one table of ten for her friends from college. Her father-in-law used their wedding as a forum to invite all sorts of business associates and, of course, the 'who's who' of the community. Actually, the Jewish community touted the wedding as 'more of a merger than a marriage,' as it was one of the social events of the year.

From the day after their marriage, her husband absolutely refused to wear his wedding ring, which hurt Candy deeply. She asked him, "If you're proud to be married to me, then why don't you wear your wedding ring?"

He said that a ring was merely a conventional tradition and that he didn't need to show others a symbol that he was married. Deeply disappointed, Candy wondered that, for someone who did not put great importance on symbols, why his writing materials had to be $1,500

Mont Blanc pens, he exclusively wore pairs of $500 Churches shoes, and his watch was an expensive Jaeger-LeCoultre.

After their marriage, Candy continued to teach grade one and helped the drama teacher present the school musicals by playing piano for the school productions. Having graduated from college two years earlier, Candy was the primary breadwinner as she was earning $11,000 a year, and her husband made very little as an article clerk in their first year of their marriage in 1978.

Even though she was given much respect and recognition as a professional teacher, she found herself to be a totally different person when she was around her controlling, arrogant husband. She learned early on that she was no match for his sarcastic, sharp comments and his critical, controlling and dominating personality. Every time she tried to express her own opinions, he would see it as a debating occasion. And when it came to debating her husband, she could never win. Instead of constantly trying to defend what she thought and having her opinions crushed, she became silent and hid her sadness behind her pretty, blue eyes.

Her silence came at a price. She allowed a pattern to be set in her very first year of marriage that would be played out for the next twenty-two years; she fed and bolstered her husband's over-inflated view of himself and failed to honour her own worth. She basically established that he was priority number one and her quiet acquiescence allowed his climbing up the corporate ladder of success to be the focus of their married life. And even though she was working as a full-time primary school teacher, rehearsing after school on musical productions and preparing lesson plans at home, she had to perform all the household duties, as he would not do anything. Simply put, his needs that had formerly been met by his mother and his family's household staff were now being met by his new wife.

Shortly after they were married, Candy received a call from her mother-in-law asking if she could come over so that they could spend the day together. Candy thought it very kind that his mother wanted to have some bonding time with her new daughter-in-law. Upon her mother-in-law's arrival, Candy noticed that she was carrying a covered basket. Her mother-in-law took out sundry ingredients needed to make meat pies. That afternoon was spent showing her new daughter-in-law how to make her son's favourite dish exactly to his liking. In this way, the transition from home to marriage would not be so traumatic for her youngest son.

Having been programmed to silence her desires, Candy did as her mother-in-law instructed and became a good, acquiescent wife. She executed her duties with silence and precision from making homemade chicken soup every Friday, to ironing the sheets and her husband's underwear. She let him establish from the start that he was king and that she was his servant.

Towards their second year of marriage, Candy found out that she was pregnant. Only weeks before, her family had moved back to America. She desperately wanted the baby to be born on U.S. soil in order that the child's citizenship would not be in question. She gave up teaching and prepared to go back to the States with her husband for the impending birth. The duration of the trip was planned to be only for the birth of the baby and, once Candy recovered, they would return to Australia. Yet this was too great to ask of her parents, as they would be miles away from their daughter and only grandchild. Blissful to have them back in the States, Candy's father spoke to his son-in-law about the possibility of obtaining a Master's Degree at the University of Virginia (UVA). The idea of possibly attending one of the most prestigious law schools in America caught the interest of his ego. He submitted his academic record, applied to complete a Master's Degree as part of the foreign lawyers' program and waited to see if he would be selected.

To help matters along, Candy's parents held a beautiful social event on their magnificent antebellum country estate, inviting notable academics from the university. One of these people was the dean of the law school. It was through the help of these connections that enabled her husband to gain admission to the university, and he started halfway through the school year. They lived in one of the houses that were on her parents' farm, which was about twenty-five minutes from UVA. From the moment that classes began, her husband was continually away at the university, leaving Candy alone with their daughter, S. He would study six days a week and take Saturdays off. Being isolated on the farm with no car, Candy knew no one and suffered terrible post-partum depression.

She had gone from having friends and colleagues, and enjoying a fulfilling career in which she received recognition, to being a stay-at-home mom in another country. Candy's terrible depression caused her to have the same recurring nightmare. Night after night, she dreamt that she would go to S's room, lift her baby out of her crib and throw her over the balcony. Horrified and ashamed, she kept this awful nightmare to herself as she thought she was going insane and that her family would commit her.

During the baby's first year, Candy tried to coax her husband to be more involved with raising their daughter and spend time with her. When he would come home from classes, Candy would be bathing S and would ask him to come in and help her. He would say, "That is your job, I'll see her after you're finished." When it came to the division of labor there were no gray areas, as he would often say, "Candy looks after the children, the house, the correspondence, the gardening, the social engagements, the washing, the cleaning - and I go to work." By this comment, it didn't appear as if he classified anything that his wife did as work.

This myopic and archaic view of married life mirrored his own father's view of domestic bliss and encouraged his emotional distance. Totally driven by work, he lost all balance in his life and missed out on his daughter's childhood experiences. In the years to follow, important moments like birthday parties, school presentations and functions, parent-teacher meetings, or important thresholds in S's life were routinely passed over for something seemingly more important in relation to his work.

His ego constantly needed feeding and his success in the law only added fuel to the fire. Totally self-consumed, he seemed to truly not be concerned with anyone else's feelings but his own. Candy actually heard him say once that he thanked all the little people he stepped on to get to where he was now.

And even though Candy knew that he was arrogant, she could not believe his constantly cruel and insensitive comments made throughout their years together. One morning in May 1980, when S was seven months old, they awoke to the radio announcer saying, "Happy Mother's Day to all you wonderful mothers out there!"

Realizing that this was her very first time celebrating Mother's Day as a new mother, Candy turned to her husband and said, "Aren't you going to wish me Happy Mother's Day?"

To which he barked back, "No, you're not my mother."

When S turned nine months old, Candy decided to take some courses at a local community college, as her mind was turning into mush. The art appreciation class was for her mind and the dance class was for her body. She would put the baby to sleep early so that, once her husband returned home from study, he didn't have to be bothered with her and Candy would race out the door. These classes made her feel alive again and restored her self-esteem.

Looking down from Heaven, Angel Ariel was elated, as she knew that by taking these courses, Claire was honoring herself and these energies would bring greater rewards into her life.

Her reward came in the form of a lovely lady by the name of Melissa, who was also taking the art class. As they chatted, they discovered that they both had nine-month-old daughters who were born within a day of each other at the same hospital. She invited Candy over to her apartment near the university, as her husband was also attending classes there. Candy proudly dressed S in the most adorable pink overalls and frilly, pink top. When Melissa opened the door to greet them, they stood speechless as they realized that the girls were dressed in exactly the same outfits. Candy loved her art class, excelled in the discussions and went on to become the top student.

At the end of the course, the students were given a choice of taking an exam or going on a bus trip to attend a lecture and tour the National Gallery of Art in Washington, D.C. Coming home excited, Candy told her husband about her upcoming class trip, which would be on a Sunday. Expressionless, he said that she would have to ask her parents to look after their daughter.

Dumbfounded, she said that he should look after her. He replied that he got one day off a week, which was Saturday, the Sabbath, and that he always studied on Sundays.

Asking him if he would make an exception, he replied, "As much as you would like it, God isn't going to move his holy day of Sabbath to suit your schedule." (Although her husband called himself an observant Jew, he chose which rules he wanted to follow and ignored most of the others as he drove on the Sabbath, turned on electrical appliances and did not eat kosher foods.)

Determined to go on the excursion with Melissa and the rest of her class, Candy asked her mother if she would look after the baby for the day. Sylvia suggested that, instead of having to ride on a cramped bus, they could all drive to Washington together. Once there, Candy could meet up with her class and when the tour began, her parents would take the baby and then meet her again after the tour and lecture had finished. Candy explained that she really wanted to go on the bus with the rest of the class. As in the past, her words fell on deaf ears; her mother said that the family would all enjoy the trip together. As this was her only option, she agreed to it. Echoes of the past seemed to come back to haunt her as she was missing out on the fun of the bus trip.

In the Great Hall of the National Gallery of Art, Candy's class was already assembled and busily chatting. Pushing S's stroller, Candy and her parents walked into the Great Hall. Melissa came over to Candy and excitedly said, "I want to introduce my husband, Troy." Blue-eyed and blonde-haired, Troy was the exact replica of their daughter, who was wiggling in his arms. Candy's heart sank. She was so jealous that, unlike her own husband, Troy had taken time off from study to look after their baby.

The lecturer waved his hands for the class to gather, as the tour was about to begin. As Candy started to move to the group, S started to scream. The huge halls of the massive museum magnified every decibel and her cries echoed throughout the building. Instead of Candy's parents taking their grandchild directly outside, they just looked at Candy and waited for her to do something. She knelt down by the stroller, hugged the baby and told her firmly that she would have to go with her grandparents. As Candy tried to stand up, S clung desperately to Candy's clothing and began to scream even louder and thrash around in the stroller. Again, Candy's parents stood frozen and didn't make any effort to take their granddaughter outside. As the uncontrollable wailing and howling continued to echo throughout the halls of the quiet museum, Candy picked S up. While she desperately tried to distract her, she noticed that her class had started to move towards the first exhibition room.

Candy quickly tried to put her back into the stroller but S's flailing arms and shrieking was making too much of a scene. As the group was getting further and further ahead, Sylvia told her just to take the baby, walk behind the group and listen. For the remainder of the tour, Candy held her squirming, squealing child, and could neither hear nor concentrate on what was being explained. It was strange how there was so much beauty housed in such wonderful halls and yet, in her crestfallen heart, Candy asked again to die.

There was something so cold and unfeeling about her husband. At times, she really wasn't sure if he had any idea how hurtful his comments were to others. Candy remembered sitting in the back of her parents' car and the subject of marriage came up. Her husband rather nonchalantly said to her father, "Hey, Len, I married your daughter under false pretenses; I thought she was rich." He not only put Candy's father down for his financial standing, but he insinuated that there was no other reason he could have possibly wanted to marry his daughter. Everyone fell deathly silent for the remainder of the trip. Often, people's silence was a result of not believing that someone could be so cruel and unkind; especially to a supposed loved one.

After finishing his Master's Degree at the University of Virginia, her husband found out that representatives of the top law firms in the U.S. flew down to UVA to interview students for jobs. He sat for an interview and was chosen to work on Wall Street at the prestigious law firm of Sullivan & Cromwell. When he told Candy that he would be accepting the position, she expressed how terribly afraid she was of living in New York City, and rightfully so.

In 1980, New York was overrun with gangs, drugs, and prostitution. Due to the violence, she asked if they could please live in the suburbs outside of the city. This would mean a one-hour train or bus commute for him to get to work. He said not to worry because he would find them a lovely place in the suburbs. After he returned from a house-hunting trip, Candy discovered that once again, her wishes had been completely ignored. He announced that they would be living in the inner city of Park Slope, Brooklyn, in an enormous apartment. New York's former mayor, Governor Carey, had previously owned this massive apartment containing four bedrooms, four bathrooms, a music room, a huge combination living and dining room, a huge kitchen, and two maid's quarters. The only problem was that this grand apartment did not come with any other maids, except Candy.

From the moment he started working at Sullivan & Cromwell, Candy hardly saw him. He would take the 6 a.m. subway to work and his average time returning home was near midnight. Apparently, working insane hours around the clock was normal for lawyers at Wall Street law firms, as they all strived to become partners.

And it would be worse when he would have to stay at the printer overseeing large runs of documents. When this happened, he would have to stay up through the night, carefully scrutinizing that the materials were printed precisely. Lawyers who worked around the clock used the term 'round robin'. This is what they called the taxi that would collect them at work, take them to their home, wait for them to quickly shower and change clothes, and then return them back to work. Lawyers on the partnership track worked continuously. Those familiar with Tom Wolfe's book *The Bonfire of the Vanities* will recall that these law firms only chose academically brilliant 4.0 valedictorians who were the best and the brightest. There is a scene at the beginning of the book where a lawyer has a heart attack and falls face first on his desk. Without missing a beat, the law firm quickly whisks him away, brings in another lawyer and business continues as usual. The following day, a small memo would be circulated around the office offering condolences with the details of the funeral service. Although seemingly funny in its lack of human connectedness, this is exactly what the law firm was like.

On the rare occasions when the spouses were invited to Sullivan & Cromwell events, Candy noted that the room was filled with so many cold and emotionless people that it seemed that they had all died but nobody had told them. Looking around the room, she remarked to one of the partner's wives that it was so lovely that many of the partners brought their daughters along. The partner's wife burst out laughing and said that these young women were, in her words, 'the partners' gifts to themselves'. She explained that many of these women, most in their twenties, were the third or fourth trophy wife, as the previous wives did not survive the Sullivan & Cromwell 'level of commitment'. Candy winced at her choice of words. Scanning these young women, many of them were barely a size 2 or 4; they were so skinny that they appeared malnourished and their vacant stares made them seem hollow and transparent.

With so many lawyers working inhuman hours to gain the coveted title of partner, one had to find a way to stand out and be noticed among so many equally brilliant and capable minds. One of the things that helped one get noticed along the partnership track was entertaining the partners and their important clients. Lawyers usually made reservations at expensive restaurants and entertained over lavish dinners. If, on the rare occasion, the partners did entertain at home, the evening was either catered or they had their maids and household staff prepare the meal.

Candy's husband announced that he had asked several important lawyers over for dinner. As she had been taught, Candy prepared a wonderful three-course gourmet meal. She set the table with beautiful, fine bone china, crystal glasses, linen tablecloth and napkins, shining silver cutlery and delicately scented flowers. After the sumptuous dinner, Candy served antique parfait glasses filled with a dessert of colorful, tiered trifle. One of the partners' wives asked if her maid was sick, as Candy was serving the dinner herself. Explaining that she did not have any maids, her guests could not believe that she had prepared the lovely meal all by herself with neither a maid to help nor a nanny to look after her child. At the evening's end, one woman who was extremely wealthy came over to Candy and said, "In appreciation of such a beautiful evening, I would like to reciprocate some time." Taking a monogrammed, silver business card holder from her purse, the woman handed Candy her card and said, "Whenever you find yourself in the city, why don't you phone me and I will take you out to lunch."

Candy stared in disbelief and felt like the woman had slapped her in the face. Yet, with her shallow and superficial nature, this woman didn't even realize how disconnected and cold her offer was. Needless to say, Candy never followed up on her invitation.

The more her husband allowed work to consume every facet of his existence, the more Candy made S the center of her universe. She started her on violin lessons at the very young age of two-and-a-half. They played duets together as Candy accompanied her on piano. Encouraging her love of color and expression, Candy set up an easel as S splashed paints onto large sheets of paper. Loving the vibrant hues and the smiling, carefree faces of her painted characters, Candy immortalized and replicated them in a series of tapestry cushions and proudly displayed them on their couch.

To foster a love of reading, every week Candy would take S in her stroller to the library and carefully select wonderful books to quench her thirst of knowledge. Using the 'Teach Your Baby to Read' method, she taught S to read fluently by the age of three. Whether it was ballet lessons or roller-skating, everything was an adventure, everything was fun, and they did everything together.

On the rare occasion that Candy would take S to the park, she had to be continually on guard against a colorful assortment of city dwellers, as the flashers, perverts and drug pushers also called the park their home. Her initial fear of living in the city was well founded, as it was a very dangerous place in the early eighties and as such, Candy kept her daughter safe by staying in their apartment. Yet, she knew that S needed friends, so she enrolled her in a playgroup called the Munchkins. This group of six children met once a week and enjoyed socializing and playtime together. The six couples would meet once a month at a different parent's house to discuss activities and trips for the group. The fathers, along with the mothers, were every bit as devoted and dedicated to their child's development; that is, all except for Candy's husband.

After pleading with him to come along and be involved in his child's life, he reluctantly came to just one of the meetings. Slumped low in his chair and sighing loudly, he did not participate in any of the discussions, visibly fidgeting during the get-together. On the way home after the meeting, Candy asked him what his thoughts were of the group. He said he spent the whole time staring at a framed photo of a pair of breasts and wondered if they belonged to the mother of one of his daughter's friends. Noting his wife's disgust, he laughed out loud and said that these parents took things way too seriously and none of this really meant anything because the children were so young.

Weeks later, the parents of the Munchkins group had organized to take the children to their first circus. The group purchased matinee tickets and they excitedly counted down the days as the date grew closer. Giving her husband enough notice to organize time off from work, he promised that he would be there. On the day, he called to say that he had been delayed and that he would meet them there. The group was sitting in a row, with the parents of each child filming their little one's excitement. S kept asking over and over where her daddy was and why he was not there. Candy kept assuring her that he would be coming soon. The circus started, eventually ended and her husband was nowhere in sight. This would be just the first of many important events that he was 'unavailable' to attend. S progressed on to kindergarten and, as fate would have it, Candy took a job as teacher's aide in her daughter's classroom. She loved working again and it gave her a sense of recognition and fulfillment that she had not experienced in a long time.

The following year, Candy was surprised to find out that her husband decided to switch to the law firm of Sidley Austin but only if he could have a position in their Washington, D.C. office. At the time, Candy thought that perhaps the move was prompted because her husband felt sorry that his wife was terrified of living in the city. Later on, she heard from friends that he had been passed over for partnership at Sullivan & Cromwell and she suspected that he had moved on to save face. No matter what the reason, Candy was elated because she and her daughter could now move away from the dangers of the city.

6

A House in the Suburbs,
A Backyard and a Dog Named Sally

Life in the peaceful suburbs of Washington, D.C., was heavenly compared to the dangers of New York City. The family now had a lovely home in a tree-lined neighborhood, with a real backyard and a little Yorkshire terrier named Sally. No sooner had they moved in than Candy's husband began travelling constantly. He swapped his routine of gruelling hours on Wall Street for commuting all over the country. He would be away four to five days out of every week and when he was in town, he continued working.

Shortly after their move, Candy had a conference with S's preschool teacher who was perplexed by a comment the child had shared when she was chosen for show and tell. She had gotten up in front of the class and proudly announced that her family had two cars; one of which was a Toyota and the other was a taxi. When the teacher asked Candy for an explanation, she told her that, with her husband's constant trips to the airport, her daughter had just assumed that the taxi was his car.

Arriving home from his business trips, Candy would ask him where he had been, as he would not inform her prior to his leaving. On one occasion, he told her that he had stayed at the exquisite Mansion at Turtle Creek in Dallas, Texas. He described the extremely beautiful women who accompanied the wealthy oil barons who stayed there, comparing their breeding to thoroughbred horses. He said that while he was having a drink at the elegant bar, one of these women tried to pick him up. Candy was upset and said that if he wore his wedding ring, it would be clear to others that he was married, to which he barked back, "I don't need to show anyone that I am married to you."

With S now enrolled in fulltime kindergarten, Candy was considering going back to work. And her prayer was immediately answered when she found out that her daughter's school was looking for a teacher to run the afterschool program. Interviewing for the job, she was hired and loved teaching again and being appreciated for her work once more. Later that year, she found out that she was pregnant, and in 1985 she gave birth to a beautiful son, J.

Every time Claire did something nurturing for herself, Angel Ariel's heart would swell with joy. Her beautiful student had connected with the understanding of the Laws of Attraction that state, '...every time we honor ourselves, the Universe then honors us'. Angel Ariel knew that a new door would open for Claire as a result of her stepping forward and honoring her gifts.

Having moved away from the city, Candy now felt a new sense of freedom. After years of hiding in her apartment from the violence of the city, she was finally able to relax with her children on their walks outside the house. While visiting a nearby park, Candy watched her daughter play with another little girl while she rocked J in his stroller. The little girl's mother, Robyn, struck up a conversation and when she found out that they were new to the area, she inquired if Candy enjoyed craftwork. Candy's face lit up and she told her that she loved to design and make tapestries. Robyn told her about a lovely group that met at her church and invited her to come along. And then she added the magic words, "They have babysitting."

Every Tuesday morning, Candy would drop S off at school and go to the nearby church. After putting J in the crèche, she found a spot at the long communal table that the crafters shared and opened a tapestry that featured an exact hand-painted replica of one of S's paintings. The other women in the group who were embroidering came over to examine Candy's handiwork. They were amazed at the accuracy and exact replication of her daughter's drawing onto the canvas.

Robyn introduced Candy to her friends Mandy, Beth and Tania. Beth asked her if she ever did tapestries for other people. Candy was about to laugh, as she had downplayed her abilities her entire life, when Beth said, "How much would you charge to make one of my daughter's drawings into a tapestry?"

Candy felt an inner push and, without thinking, she replied, "The average price for one of my tapestries is $80, but the price is dependent upon the size." She did not know where she found the courage to say such a thing, but that is all that these ladies needed to hear.

In the following year, Candy created her in-home business, Candy Crafts, and hand painted children's drawings onto canvas and made them come alive in tapestry. With each child's drawing being an original, it was a unique treasure and they were either framed or made into keepsake pillows. After both her children were settled for the night, she would sew late into the evenings. She had established friends and a small home business and decorated her new house with warmth and love. Yet, this happy chapter of her life's story would be short-lived.

As S was beginning first grade the following year, her husband discovered that the prestigious Charles E. Smith Jewish Day School was located in Rockville, Maryland, a forty-five-minute bus ride away. Desiring to send S to this well-known school, her husband decided to sell their home against Candy's wishes, uprooted the family once more, and bought a two-acre property with a large colonial home and sweeping lawns in Gaithersburg, Maryland.

Once again, Candy had to say goodbye to her friends, her support system and the beautiful life she had created to move to a new home in a new area.

Unfortunately, as they lived so far out of town, and were not on a main bus line, Candy could not get anyone to travel out so far to help her clean such an enormous house. In addition to her home duties, she was also the gardener. Every fall she planted thousands of daffodils and tulip bulbs that would burst with color in the spring. Hoping to improve the look of the neglected grounds of their new home, she pulled down the rotting fences in front of the house and whitewashed the other fences around the property. Looking up from her paint-splattered hands, she saw that the late afternoon sun was setting low in the sky. Wiping the sweat from her forehead after several hours of painting, she called the children to come in for bath time and prepared herself for another evening of being alone.

Angel Ariel watched as, night after night, Claire slept alone while her husband was away on endless business trips. A shiver went through Angel Ariel as she saw her student's once-bright face now etched with a look of resignation at the life she was living. It seemed that every time she made friends or created something that nurtured her soul, her husband would rip the rug from beneath her and move the family to start all over again. Angel Ariel knew that, on a higher level, Claire had contracted for her husband's inconsiderate actions in order to present her with great contrast for her to learn to honor and respect herself. It was not the accumulated years of abuse and disregard that would determine whether Claire would be strong enough to demand respect, but it would be her free will to decide whether she made her own needs a priority.

The year J turned one, he began to develop severe asthma. On many occasions, his attacks would come in the middle of the night. Since her husband was rarely home, there were many snowy winter nights that Candy had to wake her daughter, bundle both children into the car and rush to the hospital. After braving the icy back-roads in the middle of the night, Candy would hurry into the emergency ward.

Holding J on the gurney as her frightened face watched him turn blue for lack of breath as he gasped for air, the doctor would give him a shot of epinephrine and, invariably, he would throw up all over her. This brought up accumulated mucus in his lungs and relieved the wheezing. Once this exercise was over, Candy would wake S, who had been dozing in the waiting room, and then inch home along the slippery roads.

Upon returning from his business trip and hearing the harrowing tales of racing to the hospital, her husband seemed unaffected and did not curtail nor alter his work schedule.

Along with J's asthma, Candy began to notice that, from an early age, he became agitated and 'out of sorts' when he was in large groups of people. Seemingly routine trips to a supermarket or shopping mall could trigger uncontrollable behavior. She found out through trial and error that if she kept him to a strict schedule and close to home, he was fine. However, as he grew older and entered kindergarten, Candy was called in for a conference with his teacher, who reported that the school psychologist had observed J, and her conclusion was that he might have Attention Deficit with Hyperactivity Disorder (ADHD). The teacher went on to say that several children in the class were exhibiting hyperactive behavior and the school suggested that they be seen by a specialist. Very concerned, Candy spoke to her husband, who insisted that only the top professional in this area was competent enough to see his son. Contacting the National Institute of Health, Candy made an appointment with one of the head specialist doctors. Unfortunately, he was booked well in advance and their appointment would not be for another three months.

During that time, Candy decided to go to the Special Needs Library, which was close to their home, and began researching ADHD. When she asked the librarian for help in finding information, she told Candy that she had received a great number of calls on this condition and there was a lot of new information. Standing before a huge shelf of books and research binders, Candy's eye seemed to be drawn to only one book. Taking it from the shelf, she sat down and opened up *Why Your Child is Hyperactive* by Dr. Ben F. Feingold.

Dr. Feingold's research aimed to determine if certain foods or food additives triggered particular symptoms. The Feingold Diet, as it was called, basically looks into the way people used to eat before 'hyperactivity' and 'ADHD' became household words. Many of these children also had a history of one or more physical problems including ear infections, asthma, sinus problems, bedwetting, bowel disorders, headaches/migraines, stomach aches, and skin disorders. While the Feingold Diet might help all the symptoms, the characteristic that responded most readily was the improvement of behavior.

Candy read that the Feingold Diet consisted of taking one's child off all artificial coloring, preservatives, flavoring and additives, aspartame and artificial sweeteners and, in particular, BHT (butylated hydroxytolune), BHA (butylated hydroxyanisole) and TBHQ (tertiary butyl hydroquinone) which are made from coal tar and butane, a petroleum derivative. She was riveted as she read testimonial after testimonial from mothers who had described the diet as a Godsend, a miracle, and a prayer answered as they saw their once out of control child brought back to normal behavior again.

At the age of five, J was still wetting the bed and, although this is not an uncommon occurrence once in a while, it happened every night. He also had very little small-motor coordination control and his hand shook terribly when he tried to write. Lastly, he became easily over-stimulated, thus sending his behavior out of control. Candy decided that, since it was several months before J's appointment with the ADHD specialist, she would implement the Feingold Diet immediately. Taking him off all synthetic and artificial ingredients, she was astounded at what happened over the next three weeks. He completely stopped wetting the bed, which boosted his self-esteem and confidence. His hand stopped shaking when he wrote and he was able to print legibly. And the greatest difference was that his hyperactivity completely disappeared.

A month after starting J on the diet, Candy dropped him off at school one day. The teacher waited until he was out of earshot, came over and gave Candy a wink and whispered that ever since he went to see the doctor, he was much calmer and so pleasant with the other children. Suddenly, Candy realized that the teacher must have thought that J was under the influence of Ritalin, and said, "He has not had his doctor's appointment yet and is not on any medication. I changed his diet and the hyperactivity disappeared." Looking at Candy as if she were speaking a foreign language, the teacher shook her head and went back to the class.

Finally, the day had come for J's appointment. Entering the doctor's office, they were told that the doctor was running a little late and to please take a seat. J sat down calmly and began to read the book that he brought along. After a few minutes, Candy looked up and saw the receptionist staring at him as he sat stock still, riveted by his book. After a thirty-minute wait, the receptionist said, "The doctor will see you now. You can ask your husband to bring J in."

It dawned on Candy that the receptionist must have seen such out of control, hyperactive behavior from other children that she could not believe that this calm little boy sitting there was the patient. Taking her son's hand, Candy said emphatically, "This is my son, J," and they walked into the doctor's office.

Once inside, J extended his hand, introduced himself to the doctor and then calmly took a seat. While reviewing the chart, the doctor had a confused look on his face as he stared at the little boy calmly sitting there. The doctor turned to Candy and said, "By looking at the school's evaluation and looking at your son's behavior now, I have to ask you what has changed in the last three months?"

Candy looked at him and said, "I'll tell you what has changed. I found the Feingold Diet and implemented it. In that time, the hyperactivity disappeared, he stopped wetting the bed, and his hand stopped shaking when he writes. Why wasn't I told about this diet?"

The doctor rolled his eyes and said, "Oh yeah, the research findings on that diet are not conclusive." Candy could not believe the closed-mindedness of this doctor and she blurted out, "Shame on you! If this diet helped even one child, parents should be told about it."

In the following days, both Candy and her husband were called in to the school for a conference with the principal and J's class teacher. And even though the doctor saw with this own eyes that their son's behavior had dramatically improved and the hyperactivity had disappeared, he sent a letter to the school highly recommending that, unless he was put on Ritalin, he would not be able to function in a normal school environment. Obviously the lure of kickbacks the doctor would receive from the pharmaceutical company was a much greater incentive than honestly conveying the dramatic improvement in the child's behavior that he had encountered.

In J's defense, Candy finally got his teacher to admit that there had been a dramatic change in his behavior, as he was no longer hyperactive. But the principal stuck to her narrow-minded view and said that, unless Candy complied with putting J on Ritalin, he would not be allowed back to school.

Candy began to cry and asked to have some time to discuss this with her husband. Leaving the room, she said to him, "We will just send J to a different school that will not judge him on his past behavior."

Her husband, who was already very upset that he had to leave work to attend a meeting at school, said, "Are you crazy? This is the best Jewish day school in Washington D.C. There is no other school for my children to go to! Just put him on the medication. I have to go to work!"

In the end, Candy was beaten down and for J to return to school, she had to put him on the psychotropic drug Ritalin. Being forced to give her child this drug, Candy watched as J's usually bubbly and bright personality was wiped away like a clean slate. Almost robotic in nature, it seemed as if he had disappeared. (But God does work in strange ways – three months after J was forced to take the drug, Candy's husband was head-hunted for a job back in Australia. Starting afresh in a new country, and still following the Feingold Diet, J soon stopped taking Ritalin, as his history of hyperactivity was no longer an issue.)

Many people asked Candy how she had persuaded her son to avoid eating foods that contained harmful, artificial ingredients. She told them that she did not want to be his warden or jailer, so she taught him to read the labels on the food packaging. Having taught him to read at the age of three, he could easily discern the meaning of harmful ingredients like BHA, BHT, and TBHQ. And she stressed that there was always an alternative that he could eat, rather than denying him the pleasurable experience of having a treat.

Candy's daily routine during the week would start by rising at 6 a.m. to clean, start laundry and try to get as much done before waking the children at seven. After she dressed and fed them, she would then drive forty-five minutes to get to S's school by 8 a.m. She would then sit with J in the car and wait until his pre-school started at nine. At noon, she picked him up, raced the forty-five minutes home for a nap, and then raced back the forty-five minutes to pick S up at 3 p.m. Following after-school activities of either ballet, violin or art lessons, Candy would make the long trip home again, make dinner, bathe the children and collapse.

Candy's husband had no idea as to how much driving she had to do in one day. After arriving back from yet another business trip, he happened to look at the odometer on Candy's car and gasped at the amount of mileage she had added. He shouted, "Where the hell are you going?" Being all-consumed with his work, he had no idea what she had to do in a typical day. Again, in *his* words, he worked and Candy did everything else.

One of those things included in the 'everything else' was looking after his large Australian family who travelled to the States for extended periods. This didn't affect him in the slightest as he was never home. On top of everything else she had to do, she now had to add tour guide to her growing list as she entertained and ferried his visiting family members to different Washington landmarks and fed them.

His family would call from Australia and announce that they were coming to stay. In most cases, they did not ask, but proclaimed triumphantly that they were travelling to the States and would be arriving on a certain date. There seemed to be a constant stream of his cousins, nieces and nephews taking advantage of free lodging, free food, and Candy the tour guide.

Not long after they moved, she received a phone call from one of her husband's nephews in Australia. He said that his sixteen-year-old sister wanted to come for a visit. Having experienced this same scenario previously, Candy asked how long she would be staying. Taking a few moments to respond, the nephew was a bit unsure and could not say. It was then that Candy asked why his sister had not made the call herself to ask if she could come and stay. He said, "She doesn't want to speak to you."

A month later, when the niece arrived, it became very clear why she was sent overseas to relatives. Having lost her beloved father at the tender age of eleven, this sixteen-year-old girl was depressed, anorexic and suicidal. Not knowing what else to do with the teenager, her family thought it was a good idea to send her away to relatives in the States. Underneath her expressionless face, this young girl held a deeply tortured sadness within, would not do anything and refused to eat. Several weeks after arriving, the niece's things started appearing in S's room. When Candy asked S about the appearance of the objects, she said that her cousin had given her teddy bear and her jewelry to her. Discussing this behavior with a friend who was a psychologist, she said it sounded like the niece was going to kill herself. Could that be the reason she was giving her things away?

In the five months that the niece remained with them, Candy encouraged her to take an exercise class and gave her the spot that Candy had paid and reserved for herself. She finally persuaded the niece to eat, and slowly she began to laugh and engage with others again. Having been nurtured and nourished back to emotional and physical wellness, the niece returned to Australia a totally different girl than when she had arrived. With all the love, encouragement, and constant care that Candy gave her niece, the turnaround in this young woman's emotional and physical well-being was never acknowledged by either her husband or the girl's family.

The heaviness that Claire experienced by allowing herself to be used saddened Angel Ariel. She had tried numerous times to get her student's attention in her dream state when she would whisper words of encouragement to her. But Angel Ariel knew full well that all the angel wishes in the Universe would not take the place of the human soul choosing to bring more happiness and joy into her own life. All she could do was to send angel signs to try to get Claire's attention. But, if there is one thing that an angel has, it is all the time in the world. When it came to guiding her assigned human's soul, Angel Ariel, like all angels, never gave up.

Rushing to get her children ready for school, Candy was surprised by an early morning phone call from a woman who introduced herself and told Candy that she had heard from her cousin, Robyn, that Candy painted and designed tapestries of children's work. She asked Candy how much she now charged for an original hand-designed tapestry. Candy quoted her a price and arranged to meet the woman. Hanging up the phone, she was quite surprised. Having put all her time into moving and resettling her family, she had not even attempted to pursue any of her creative efforts. Thinking about the phone call, she smiled and began to get excited about re-establishing her home-based business.

Sensing the rise in Claire's energies and a lifting of her spirit, Angel Ariel breathed a sigh of relief. It had been a good idea of hers to arrange for this new customer to call Claire and remind her of how much she missed nourishing her creative joy.

Angel Ariel's inspiration could not have been better timed, as J was starting pre-school. With the extra time to herself, Candy decided to take a room in their house and turn it into an art studio. Remembering the overwhelming response that she had had creating her tapestry pillows for others, she began to take her own children's drawings and fabric-painted them onto T-shirts. With both her children proudly wearing their designs to school, the other moms asked Candy where she had bought the shirts. This lead to making unique T-shirts with other children's designs in addition to her commissioned needlework projects. Her gift and whimsy in her art also saw her branching out to painting her illustrations on children's furniture. Her Candy Crafts business provided an outlet for her creativity and nourished her soul.

As Christmas was fast approaching, she had bought baskets and was painting and decorating them to give away as presents. With all of her husband's moneyed colleagues and clients, she thought to offer them an opportunity to order Christmas baskets as corporate gifts. Slowly, her art studio began to look like Santa's workshop as she bought Camembert and Brie wheels, bottles of Champagne, fine water crackers and imported jellies and jams to fill the baskets. Some of them had hand-painted lyrics to Christmas carols and others had ribbons and bells intertwined with green holly and lovely poinsettias wrapped in tinsel.

And while Candy adored her business, the time devoted to filling her art and craft orders came on top of her already full schedule with long hours spent in the car, her household duties, gardening and tending to her children. The balance of duties could have been made more equitable, as the 1980s gave birth to the super woman. With women going back to work, it forced men to shoulder some of the responsibilities of child rearing and household duties. Well, it forced *some* men to take on responsibilities. Her husband was brought up very differently. According to his upbringing, child rearing and house cleaning was a woman's job. After a meal, he would not even take his plate and put it in the sink. He would get up and leave the dishes for 'the wife' to clean up, because that was her job. He was brought up in a household where women were not only subservient but were treated like second-class citizens. He was legendary for putting down females. His sarcastic, biting comments about women being less capable than men did not go over well with his female colleagues at his new law firm in Washington. They threatened him with a sexual harassment suit, which quieted his tongue, yet only when he was around the office.

It seemed amazing how disconnected and unconcerned her husband was with anything that affected his family. Of all the callous and cold-hearted things her husband did, there was one in particular that stood out. A very wealthy friend, an Australian investor, phoned to tell her husband that he and his wife were coming to Washington and wanted to be introduced to possible business contacts for future investments.

Wanting to make a good impression, Candy's husband announced that he had invited the couple to come for dinner the following night. Candy stood speechless, not believing what she had just heard. Both the children had been suffering from flu and fever for several days and she had had very little sleep tending to them both. She told him to take the couple out to a restaurant for dinner. But he said it would make a much better impression if she would make dinner at home. With both children ill, Candy managed to shop, clean the house, make a beautiful dinner and set a full table with the china, pressed linen, crystal wine glasses and shining silver service.

After picking up his friend and his spoiled, indulged wife from their hotel, her husband arrived home around 6:30 p.m. and quickly arranged drinks for his guests. Candy introduced both children, who were in their robes, and said she would put them to bed, as they had been ill for several days.

After settling S and J, Candy re-entered the kitchen, just in time to hear the investor say, "...well, if all those business people are going to be at that Christmas party tonight, then we definitely should be there as well. Think of all the people we are going to meet there." Leaving the room, her husband brought them their coats and the couple and her husband left. There was no apology, no dinner. Nothing.

Candy sat alone for the longest time in paralyzed silence, too frozen to cry, as she watched the candles burn down in the carefully polished candlesticks on the beautifully set table.

With her son entering first grade, Candy decided to go back to school to get her degree in graphic design. Living far out of town, she had no idea how she would be able to accomplish this. Yet, as luck would have it, a family had recently moved onto the neighboring property and their daughter was enrolled at the same school as S and J.

Of course, it was Angel Ariel who had arranged for the meeting with this little girl's mother. Claire did not realize it at the time, but because of the Laws of Cause and Effect, every time she honored herself, the angels honored her with something that would foster her desires.

Candy asked the little girl's mother if she would take S and J to school on the mornings that she had class and Candy would bring them all home every afternoon. She decided to take only two classes a semester because she had to fit her studies and projects in with all her other 'wifely' duties. During an entire year of study, she still did all her household chores, as her husband never once amended his schedule or work in any way to consider or accommodate her pursuits. After the first year, all four of her grades put her on the dean's list and she was looking forward to her second year at college, but fate would step in yet again.

It was during this time, when Candy was feeling so much better about herself, that her husband announced that, through a friend of his, they had the opportunity to invest in the last privately-owned movie theater company in the States, which included eight theaters and thirty-five screens in the Washington, D.C., area. He found out about this great opportunity from a friend who was in the movie business. It was decided that, because he was working full time as a partner in a law firm, he would take on the title of CEO, his friend would be president of the company and Candy would be VP. She told her husband that she wanted to finish her graphic design degree, but he told her that she would be able to dress up every day, have her own office, and it would be so much fun working in the movie business. He added that, since he was still a law partner, she would have to be his eyes and ears to watch over the business. Being programmed to follow her husband's dictates, she reluctantly put her own wishes aside and denied her heart's longing.

In addition to already being burdened with living on a property a great distance from town, looking after an asthmatic child and having no help to look after their large home, Candy now had to also fit in a full time job at the theater office.

It was common knowledge that many of the partners' wives at her husband's law firm lived on similar large properties and had live-in help. With the increased workload, she mustered up enough courage to ask to employ help once again. Never having given any consideration to assisting his wife in their ten-year marriage with the immense workload that she was carrying, Candy's pleas fell on deaf ears again. So, she just found more hours in the day by getting up earlier, at 5 a.m., to clean, do laundry and prepare meals before going to bed after midnight.

The main office of the movie theaters was in Chevy Chase, a very prestigious area of Washington, D.C. Candy would park her car in the garage of a nearby shopping mall that housed one of their theaters. As she walked through the mall, she noticed that there were groups of senior citizens who exercised in the mall before the stores opened. They were not shopaholics, they simply feared for their lives if they were to walk the violent, crime-ridden city streets of Washington in the 1990s. With many of the stores opening at 9:30 a.m., the seniors had to be finished with their exercise by this time. When Candy mentioned the marching senior citizens group to her husband, this gave him an idea. He noted that their theater in the shopping mall did not open until 11:30 a.m. He proposed that they open the theater every Wednesday for seniors and that Candy run this special screening. And that is how the Nostalgic Film Club was born.

Candy advertised, researched and canvassed senior citizen groups in the area and it turned out that Chevy Chase had a large retirement population. In addition to coordinating buses for the senior citizens to come to the theater, she set about contacting Ted Turner's organization, which had bought up many of the film rights for well-known, classic movies. She then booked films such as *Three Coins in the Fountain, Bringing Up Baby* and *An Affair to Remember*, and soon, she had a lovely schedule of dates and old movies booked for delivery throughout the upcoming year. For the special low price of $3.50, the seniors would receive a ticket, a small popcorn and a drink.

As Candy arrived for the opening of the Nostalgic Film Club at 9:30 a.m., she was pleasantly surprised to see many seniors waiting in line. Introducing herself to the group, she helped them to their seats, as many of them had walkers or were in wheelchairs. Once they were all settled in the theater, Candy did a final head count: twenty-four customers. She was quite encouraged as they were only one person shy of breaking even. As the plush burgundy curtains began to part and the beautiful music started to play for the opening film, *Three Coins in the Fountain,* this older generation was swept back in time to another place and era. At the end of the film, the house lights came on, and Candy positioned herself by the exit to farewell the seniors and present them with a flyer announcing next week's movie presentation.

Among the seniors was a tiny, white-haired lady who slowly made her way up the aisle and stopped in front of Candy. She had tears running down her cheeks and reached out and held Candy's hand in her wrinkled hands. Concerned that something had happened to upset her, Candy said, "My dear, what is wrong?"

The elderly lady looked at Candy and her whole face broke into a smile. "You have no idea what you have done for me. The first date I was ever allowed to go on was to the movies to see this one. I remember being very self-conscious as I inspected my gloves and hoped that my hat was on straight. When the theme music started, I looked over excitedly at my very handsome date, Bill, who would later become my husband. Although he passed away many years ago, when I heard that same theme music today, I was transported back to that time of first love. I can't thank you enough. God bless you, my dear."

Every Wednesday, Candy would arrive at the movie theater and see the beaming faces of the seniors as they waited in line. With each passing week, they felt more and more comfortable with Candy. Many of them, lonely and isolated from their families, would take Candy into their confidence, telling her about their sons and daughters, their grandchildren, their loved ones who had passed away, and the stories of their lives and memories.

No matter how much advertising Candy did, the numbers for the Nostalgic Film Club never seemed to rise above twenty-four people. With the audience being elderly, it was very difficult to build numbers, as many of them would not be able to attend due to illness or surgeries. There were even a few regulars who passed away during the time of the film club. Candy would report how successful the club was, as the seniors loved her choice of films and loved her. Once again missing the human element, and choosing to see life only from the bottom line, her husband commented that it would only be a success if they could break even. As far as Candy was concerned, seeing the seniors' faces beam was success enough for her.

In the end, it turned out that the movie theater chain was a failing business and whatever money it made was slipping through the fingers of other people associated with it. Candy was never told how much money they actually lost, but by his reaction, she figured it must be quite substantial. And she never did get the chance to finish that graphic design degree, but life had other things in store for her.

Her husband was hit with another blow after the failed movie business venture. The recession of the early 1990s took a toll on law partners, as many lost their jobs. Apparently partners didn't have tenure like university professors and could be laid off. Desperately looking for a position, he learned about an Australian company looking for an Australian lawyer with overseas experience to help them build an in-house legal department. And, as they say, the rest was history. With a heavy heart, Candy moved to Melbourne, Australia, in 1993. She and her children had lived in the Washington area for the past eleven years and had made many lovely friends. It was with great sadness that she found herself moving to the other side of the world again.

7

Back in a Foreign Land

Each time her husband decided to move, Candy felt like a plant that has been uprooted. For the first few times, it will suffer the trauma of having its roots ripped up and it will put all its efforts into recouping its strength to thrive in its new environment. But when a plant is ripped from its foundation over and over again, it weakens each time it is transplanted and it becomes even more difficult to adapt to its new surroundings.

Unlike previous moves where Candy was able to bounce back and create a life for herself, this time she felt utterly alone and lost and she became depressed. Just the opposite was true for her husband, who was fully engaged with his increased work commitments and seemed to thrive in his prestigious new role as chief lawyer. With no family or friends for support, Candy felt as if she was adrift, abandoned on a lonely sea and her husband was so consumed with his work that he did not notice his wife's spiralling sadness.

Like a well-trained soldier, Candy did exactly what was expected of her: she created a lovely home for her family and attended to her children's needs, all while she was dying inside. Settling fourteen-year-old S and eight-year-old J into their new country, she set about making friends with the moms at school. Arriving early to pick up her children, she scanned the playground for a friendly face to strike up a conversation. After several days of trying to introduce herself, she experienced distracted smiles and half-hearted attempts to engage with her. These women were not interested in inviting anyone new into their circle of friends.

Without a support system to help her, she became disheartened and felt defeated. She wanted desperately to go back to work or study, but this was not an option as the children's daily care had always been solely her responsibility. And while many of her husband's associates had childcare as their wives worked or studied, her husband adamantly refused to pay for someone else to look after his children. He already had a servant.

Throughout her married life, Candy's parents were not blind to how terribly sad their daughter had become. Even though they had experienced being on the receiving end of their son-in-law's cold, heartless comments, they figured that their daughter was financially secure and never mentioned anything to her. Perhaps her parents sensed the severity of Candy's unhappiness, which prompted them to plan a trip to Australia the following year. It was with great excitement and joy that Candy received the news of her parents' arrival and she planned a wonderful dinner for them.

Gathered for the traditional Friday night Sabbath dinner, the family listened to Candy's husband say the blessing over the wine and bread, and welcomed this lovely day of peace and rest. As the first course was served, her husband looked across the table at Len, pointed to Candy and said, "I bet you are thankful that at least one of your children turned out to be normal."

Candy's father, who so deeply adores all of his children, turned white with disbelief and was unable to speak as he stared at his son-in-law. Sylvia very tactfully took her napkin from her lap, quietly placed it on the table, turned to her husband and said, "Leonard, I have a headache, we have to go now."

Candy was crushed as the beautiful evening she had planned for her parents was ruined. Chasing after them, she implored her parents to stay. Kissing their daughter goodbye, they said that they would phone the next day. Re-entering the kitchen, Candy saw that her husband had not missed a beat and went right on eating his soup. When others would comment how beautiful and talented Candy was, her husband would reply, "Of course she is; she's married to the perfect man."

With their move to Australia in 1994, Candy's husband's work hours and commitments increased, as did his time spent out of the country. He travelled so much that he boasted he was the second-most travelled person in Australia as he was on a plane more often than he was on the ground. The constant ache and loneliness for recognition and love created a hollow void in Candy's life.

Looking down from Heaven, Angel Ariel watched as Claire blankly stared out the window. With each previous move, Claire had managed to muster up some shred of optimism and tried to find her feet again after resettling. But this time, there was an expressionless resignation that haunted her and caused Angel Ariel even greater concern. She saw Claire's soul withering and losing the will to live.

To fill that void, Candy nurtured herself with a growing addiction to shopping. Her husband's larger salary afforded her the increased limit on her credit card and the expensive, fashionable stores of Toorak and South Yarra, Melbourne, were right in her backyard. The more her shopping expeditions increased, the more the owners of the boutiques gave her a welcoming reception every time she and her credit card entered their store. Starved for attention, Candy thought that the storeowners genuinely liked her, but what they liked most was that she spent a lot, and often.

Having clothed herself in designer chic, she turned her attention to her body. Joining a trendy gym and dressed in designer exercise outfits, she proceeded to whittle her body down from a size 10 to a size 4. Her issues with food control increased and her anorexic body weight hovered around 100 pounds. She exercised six days a week, often staying at the gym for three to four hours. Although beautiful on the outside, she was desperately empty on the inside, longing for companionship and attention. What she craved most was someone to spend quality time with.

Arriving home from work one day, her husband announced that he had been chosen to attend an exclusive, executive retreat program for two months at Insead Business School in France. Assuming that this trip was meant for the families as well, Candy excitedly suggested that S could stay with any number of her many friends and that she and J could enrol in French classes during the day. He quickly quashed her excitement, telling her that the program did not allow spouses and children to attend.

Before he left on his trip, Candy told him that she had always wanted a Chanel suit. She figured that if she wasn't going to France, then she could ask for something very nice instead. Describing the suit in detail and writing down her measurements, Candy told her husband that she would like a pastel-coloured suit that was either light blue, pink or yellow, perhaps featuring ribbons and bows. In her description of the suit she stressed two important things – nothing patterned and nothing green.

Arriving home two months later, her husband presented the family with gifts. Candy was so excited when she saw the beautifully wrapped box from a fashionable boutique. Opening the box, she took out a size 12 suit that was bright Kelly green with large, red poinsettias splashed all over it. At first she thought it was a joke. Incredulous, she asked him whom this suit was for. He said that the beautiful Parisian girls in the store had questioned him as to what his wife's tastes were and her size in order for them to select just the right suit. By his description of her tastes, they chose something patterned and green that was three sizes too big. It pained her so much to look at the hideous suit, the physical representation of how little regard her husband had for her, that she ended up giving it away to Goodwill.

The suit was one of the endless examples of her words falling on deaf ears, as he had never really listened to nor acknowledged her desires before. In fact, during their first year of marriage she had hinted at the present she would like for her upcoming birthday. Her husband's abrupt reply was that she was not allowed to ask for the present she wanted, as it would ruin the surprise. Invariably he would forget her birthday altogether or remember at the last minute and get his secretary to run out and buy Candy some bath soaps. The sadness and sting of not being regarded nor important enough for her desires to be considered soon were added to the accumulated sadness already heavy on her heart.

With Christmas fast approaching, the usual rounds of party invitations started to come in the mail. Arriving at a gathering hosted by one of her husband's colleagues, they entered the beautiful, lavishly decorated home filled with people. On top of the shining ebony grand piano, Candy noticed quite a number of photos on display of the partner, his wife and their children. The wife of her husband's colleague came over and picked up a photo of herself and her two children in front of the Eiffel Tower. She said, "Candy, these were taken when we went along to France for the Insead program. Who could possibly pass up an all-expense-paid trip to France? The children and I had such fun learning French and sightseeing." Discovering that wives and families had actually been allowed to go and that her husband had lied to her, Candy felt a wave of nausea come over her. She bit the inside of her lip and forced a smile as another piece inside of her died.

In 1996, the news of a devastating volcanic eruption would introduce Candy to the publishing world. Her parents had owned a vacation home in the Caribbean for many years on the island of Montserrat. When they lived in the United States, Candy and her family would visit the island for several weeks over the Christmas holidays. Being a keen photographer, her husband loved taking photos of the beautiful island. The towering volcano Mount Soufriere had been dormant for six hundred years and in 1996, it decided to erupt and come alive again. With the devastation on the island and the whole town destroyed, Candy's family was now in possession of photos of the island's buildings and landmarks that no longer existed. It was decided that Candy would take her husband's photographs and the beautiful poems her father had written about the island, and marry them into a coffee table book entitled *Montserrat – The Emerald Isle.*

This project saw her overseeing all aspects of the book, including designing the layout. When the book was finally completed, she undertook its marketing and visited bookstores in the Melbourne area. To promote the book, she even appeared on the very popular Australian television show *Good Morning Australia,* with host Bert Newton. Sales of the book were active as long as the volcano was erupting and featured in the news. Yet, the moment that the volcano was dormant again, sadly the book sales began to die down.

When her husband heard the news of the book sales dropping, he became infuriated. For as much as he loved having his ego stroked by seeing his photography featured in a coffee table book, he would have preferred to earn a profit on his investment from the publishing of the book. He decided that he would organize a fundraising activity with the Rotary Club with a percentage of the sale of each book going to a fund for the displaced children of the island. He then gave Candy a long list of well-heeled, wealthy professionals – bankers, lawyers and doctors – and presented her with copies of a cover letter explaining about the fund for the children of the island. The book would then be enclosed with the letter asking the recipients if they would like to contribute to the fund – in other words, buy the book.

At first, Candy thought it was very presumptuous to send people a book and make them feel guilty and obligated to purchase it to help with the charity. She explained to her husband how uncomfortable she felt sending the books and the letter. He barked at her, "You choose how you feel about it, but send out those God-damned envelopes; I want my money back!"

In the end, most of the people were touched that a percentage of the book's proceeds were to go to the displaced children's fund and they bought the book. However, there were several people who sent the book back, saying, "How dare he have the affront to ask for a contribution in this manner?"

Because her husband looked after all the finances, Candy never was privy to how much he garnered from those book sales and how much was actually given to the children's fund, although she always surmised that there was no fund and the only thing funded by this whole exercise was the lining of her husband's pockets.

Although Candy allowed herself to be controlled over the twenty-plus years of marriage, she never stopped loving her husband and never gave up trying to rescue the relationship. Throughout their marriage, she would become so desperate for him to spend time with her that she suggested different activities that they could share. She had such little self-worth that she honestly believed that just being together with her did not hold enough enticement.

In their first year of marriage, she coaxed him into participating in Chinese cooking classes. She bought the wok, the utensils, and sesame seed oil and booked in for a twelve-week course. He made it to the first lesson and then his work commitments took precedence again, not just for one week but for the remainder of the course. Because Candy suggested the cooking lessons in order for them to spend quality time together, she decided not to go without her husband. Their cooking lessons were severely 'underdone'.

Later that year, desperate to make another attempt, she suggested they attend lectures that their Rabbi was giving on ancient Egyptology. Looking back, it was not so much the activity that mattered, it was the time spent together that she craved. They attended one lecture and because of his work commitments the rest of the lectures were, pardon the expression, 'ancient history'.

Being the eternal optimist, Candy decided to book a series of squash lessons for both of them. Again, by the second lesson, another business trip took priority and the lessons were 'squashed'. Again, Candy gave up and refused to continue on her own. So in 1996, singing the same old song to her husband of, 'We never do anything together', Candy suggested that they take Italian classes. They loved the food, the culture, and the country. Buoyed along by yet another possibility of bonding, she organized Italian lessons at a language school in the city that was very close to her husband's office, where they could meet after he finished work. After attending the first class, armed with homework, she felt enthusiastic about learning this beautiful language. A few days before their next class, another business trip reared its head. He told her to go, take the lessons and she could teach him what he missed. Absolutely seething, Candy decided to cancel the lessons. This time, however, unlike all the other times, something changed inside of her. She came to the conclusion that, for the first time, she would see herself as an independent person and continue the class without her husband; simply for her own enjoyment.

Choosing to attend these classes by herself, she felt a lifting of her spirit and a renewed spark of light warming her heart. It was then that she decided that she would not only attend the classes, but would take it on as a quest to speak Italian better than Italians as revenge for her husband continually cancelling on her.

At Claire's decision to finally do something solely for herself after twenty years of marriage, Angel Ariel flew into the air with her heart filled with joy. She had desperately wanted to help her beautiful friend to empower herself, yet being unable to interfere with free will, all she could do was to whisper words of strength and encouragement to help her to be brave and to choose to be happy. Angel Ariel felt elated by Claire's choice and she lovingly sent prayers that she would continue to build on this independence and see herself as deserving and worthy of asserting her wishes and desires.

Not only did Candy attend classes, but her every waking second was dedicated to learning the language. Armed with headphones and a Walkman, she studied Berlitz language tapes at home while cooking, vacuuming, scouring the bathrooms and while running errands in the car. Within no time, Italian books, music and recipes started to take over the house as she ate, slept and breathed all things Italian. The sounds of the Italian radio station were a constant in their home as she listened throughout her day. Full of confidence, she entered one of their quizzes and actually beat two other contestants, Maria Gratzia and Catarina, in their native language!

She studied and immersed herself with such intensity that by the end of the first year, she had a reasonable fluency in the language. And although she was ecstatic at her expertise she had no one with whom to practice. Fortunately, with Melbourne having such a huge population of Italians running and working at the various green grocers and supermarkets, she would travel to the city's northern suburbs to shop and converse with the locals.

Armed with a fiery determination to speak the language like a native, Candy acquired a natural grace and ease of conversing. At corporate functions that she would attend with her husband, there were a few partners who spoke Italian and she was congratulated as she brazenly showed off her newfound ability. Her husband looked on helplessly as his wife was holding the attention and focus for the first time in their married life. This attention whetted her appetite to find more willing participants to converse with and create more opportunities to speak Italian.

Having gone just about as far as she could go with ordering her groceries and participating in talkback Italian radio, she decided to broaden her horizons. She placed an ad in the local paper to start a conversation meet-up group. The ad, written in English, asked for people to call a voice mail number and listen to the message recorded in Italian. If their language proficiency was advanced enough to understand the message, then they would be able to follow the instructions on how to contact Candy in order to join the group. Having reached an advanced level herself, she wanted to weed out those who had less than excellent conversation skills. Within a short time, the voice mailbox became full of messages from people eager to join.

She also asked callers to leave their message in Italian and tell her a little about themselves. After careful selection, she chose five people to join her group and arranged for them to meet at a different Italian restaurant each Tuesday. She was so nervous meeting the members of the group for the first time. There were four people out of the five participants who were second generation Italians: Paolo and Gabriella were newly engaged, Alessandra was a pretty young hairdresser, and Tony, who worked in a warehouse and was always quick to point out his amazing prowess with the opposite sex. Some would say typically Italian, yet he was a really nice fellow and totally harmless. Completing the group was John, a huge Dutchman who had an uncanny resemblance to John Candy. He already spoke four other languages and was adding Italian to his list. It didn't take long for the little group to bond and Candy really looked forward to each Tuesday night.

After several months, she decided to put another ad in the paper, to see who else she could entice to join the group. Within no time, the little group was to be little no more. There were so many people who wanted to join that Candy found herself booking restaurants in advance and organising members. After six months, there were too many members for one group, so she decided to split the groups; those under forty-five years old and those over.

Although Candy herself was only forty-two at the time, she went along to the first meeting of the older group and was elated to meet such vibrant, passionate people. Retirees with new leases on life, they chose to learn Italian and were very grateful that Candy had organized a conversation meet-up. A few months later, she received a call from a widow in the group who had announced her engagement to one of the gentlemen whom she had met at this group. She blessed and thanked Candy for changing her whole life and invited her to the wedding. And, of course, their wedding was held at the Italian Club.

Another result of her efforts was that her husband was thrilled; not that his wife was doing something that she enjoyed, but that she had finally stopped nagging him about never spending time together. He was all-consumed with himself and his work and he never gave anything outside of himself much thought at all. His workload and travel increased to such inhuman levels that his health began to suffer as he climbed the never-ending ladder of success.

Due to his enormous work schedule, it was quite common for Candy and her husband to go in separate cars when he invited friends and colleagues to restaurants or concerts. Many times, he would either leave half way through or just not turn up at all, leaving Candy to play social secretary with his invited guests. In the two years that they had lived in Australia, having sold his soul to the self-induced pressures of obtaining success, power and money, Candy had watched her husband's hair turn grey; he packed on thirty extra pounds and his skin took on the pallor of old, grey hamburger meat.

Arriving home from running errands on a weekday, Candy heard noises coming from the second floor. Knowing that her husband would work even if he were dead and that he never came home during the day, Candy thought the house was being robbed. Slowly creeping up the stairs, she peered into their bedroom, and was shocked to see her husband in bed. He was talking on the land line and mobile phone at the same time and had his computer on his lap as he answered emails. Candy watched in disbelief, as every ten minutes his back would start to spasm. Grimacing in pain, he would stop momentarily until the pain subsided, at which point he would start working and speaking once again.

Alarmed at how pale and ill he had become, she said to him, "Stop what you are doing, hang up the phones; you're killing yourself." He angrily hushed her and kept on working.

Not fully knowing where it came from, Candy plucked up enough courage to say, "You are going to come home one day and I won't be here." He sneered and spat at her, "Where would you go? You have no options and nobody would ever want you."

Even with this kind of treatment, Candy still felt so sorry for him. In the following week, she called his office early in the morning and remarked that, since it was such a beautiful day, they should meet for lunch. Arranging to meet at his office at noon, Candy dressed beautifully and drove into the city. As she walked to his building, she stopped and bought him a long stemmed red rose. Arriving a little early, Candy was greeted by his loyal secretary, Elizabeth, who said that she wasn't sure where he was but he should be back soon, as he knew about their lunch date. Candy waited patiently for over an hour. There was no phone call, no apology – nothing. In the end, horribly embarrassed and deeply saddened, she put the rose on his desk and walked out. This was the beginning of allowing herself to imagine life completely without him.

Week after week, she would excitedly look forward to going out with her Italian group. She would watch other couples enjoying each other's company and she silently wished and longed for a similar experience; someone to spend quality time with, someone who would take an interest in her.

As part of entertaining important clients, her husband often bought subscription tickets to the Concert Hall. Yet, because of work commitments, he would be unable to attend the beautiful theatre and musical events. Having experienced a life in which her husband let her down time and time again, Candy had refused to go without him and many times, these tickets would go unused. Yet it was after being stood up at his office that she decided that she would go to the next concert on her own.

Standing in the foyer of the beautiful Melbourne Concert Hall, she sipped a drink before the concert. Once again, her eyes were drawn to couples who were enjoying the evening together. Tears welled up in her eyes as she longed to have someone special with whom to share the evening. Although Mozart was a favourite composer of hers, she might as well have been deaf because she didn't even hear the music. Looking down at the empty seat beside her, she felt a great wave of sadness and huge tears streamed down her face.

Angel Ariel looked down from Heaven and saw clearly the path that was unfolding for her beautiful student. She had watched every step of Claire's life unfold since she had moved to Melbourne and she knew that the emptiness in her heart was a huge wake-up call for her to make changes in order to step forward to a more honouring life.

Knowing that her husband would be unable to use the next month's tickets, she started to think how much fun it would be to have a friend to invite along. Having had such wonderful success with her Italian group, she decided to combine her love of Italian with finding a friend and composed an ad to be featured in the local paper. It read:

'Bright lady with a fun sense of humour is searching for an Italian friend – between the ages of 35 and 50 – to go to the theatre, movies and concerts, must speak Italian. Must be well read, have knowledge of the cultural arts and also have a sense of humour. Please listen to my voicemail and reply in Italian.'

It didn't take long for the calls to come in. Yet, Candy was so surprised that all the calls were from men; she had not specified that she was looking for a girlfriend. Many of the messages were sleazy in nature and, naturally, they were left unanswered. Yet there was a singular message that had a soft, gentle and inviting tone that caught Candy's attention and she arranged to meet with this gentleman at a busy restaurant on Lygon Street in Melbourne's inner city. As they sat down for lunch, there was an ease of conversation in Italian and they laughed a lot. They both had a love of long black coffee and cigarettes. Candy had recently started smoking again after having given up for fifteen years and felt a sense of defiance in beginning again.

R was thirty-one years old and a body builder who worked in construction. He said he had never read the local paper before, yet he felt drawn to read the ads this one time. He was tired of all the 'games' women played in relationships and thought that it was so refreshing that she was simply looking for someone to share cultural evenings with, as he was particularly enamoured with opera. The more they spoke, the more they discovered that they had similar tastes in movies, and she was certainly surprised about how much he was in touch with his feminine side. He knew just about every romantic comedy and his eyes misted over when he spoke about movies like *The Bridges of Madison County* and *Return to Me.* This was so foreign to Candy because living with her husband's emotional constipation for twenty-two years often saw them watching war movies and action films.

Her husband had professed that his favourite movie of all time was *Lawrence of Arabia* because it did not have any women in it and that it was violent. Candy recalled watching *The Great Escape* on their honeymoon night! Even R's taste in music had a softer leaning, as he spoke about his preference for The Carpenters and Celine Dion.

As their afternoon drew to a close, they both agreed that they enjoyed each other's company and decided to meet again. Although Candy rationalised that he was only a friend, she never told her husband about R. When it came to her husband's consideration of her wishes over the past twenty-two years, his words and actions were anything but accepting.

Over their long marriage, her husband had systematically bullied her and belittled any shred of self-worth that she might have had. He used to say that her friends were losers and that she listened to 13th century 'evil music', his description of Baroque music. He often told her that when he first met her, she was a peasant like her mother, and it was he who took full credit for making her a lady. This constant mocking of her character and tastes erased any willingness to share her newfound friendship with her husband.

She invited R to come along to the Tuesday evening Italian conversation group. He fit in with the rest of the group and everyone enjoyed his great sense of humour. One of the things that Candy noticed was how well dressed R was all the time. His attention to fashion was remarkable. He took note of the textures in materials, the tones and shading of colours and how well items coordinated with each other. From the first day they met in May 1998, Candy and R felt like long-lost best friends.

Looking down from Heaven, Angel Ariel knew full well why Claire felt this way about R. Theirs was a karmic connection, as he was part of her soul group and had contracted to help her. In order to grow spiritually, Angel Ariel knew that Claire needed to leave her dishonouring marriage and the callousness of her husband. In addition, she knew that Claire had become so disempowered by her marriage that it would never have occurred to her to leave on her own. This is why Angel Ariel called in the deep love of a soul mate to help her to leave.

In June 1998, Candy summoned up the courage to ask her husband for a separation. As the summer holidays were coming up, she rented a house by the beach and he booked a holiday with J. It was during those three weeks away that Candy wrestled with the decision of whether to continue her marriage or ask for a divorce. At the end of the three weeks, she found herself no closer to a final decision. Yet on her return, she had other things to divert her attention.

For the past six months, she had been organising all the details for J's Bar Mitzvah. The next few weeks would see the preparations of the catering, venue, decorations, speeches and guest list seating all primed and ready for the big day. For this wonderful ceremony of a boy's coming of age, her husband's family had flown from Perth to Melbourne a week early to spend time with them. Well, that is, spend time with Candy, as her husband never made himself available to spend any quality time with any of his family, knowing that Candy would play hostess and tour guide as usual.

One sunny morning, she decided to show her mother-in-law and her sister-in-law the beautiful markets in South Yarra. Timing their arrival at 11 a.m., they chose a delicious selection of freshly baked pastries and sat in a sun-drenched palazzo for morning tea. Although Candy felt especially close to both of them, she had never spoken openly about her great sadness in her marriage. Yet as they sat down to have tea, there was something inside Candy that was urging her to finally open up to them.

As she began to speak, her voice trembled and huge tears streamed down her face. Gathering up her courage, she spoke about the years of bullying, the belittling comments, the emotional abuse and her life of being treated like a servant. As she spoke honestly and emotionally, revealing the raw pain deep in her heart, both women sat stone-faced, emotionless, and unaffected by what Candy was divulging.

As she finished speaking, Candy looked up at her mother-in-law through her swollen, tear-stained eyes. Calmly taking a sip of tea, her mother-in-law spoke in a very cold, matter-of-fact manner. "Yes, this is the curse that all the women in this family must bear and each of us deals with it in our own way." Having been mentally, emotionally and physically abused, she pointed to herself, and added, "I have dealt with it my way." She had become an acquiescent, silent observer, afraid to voice her own opinions in order to avoid the wrath and anger of her husband. She then pointed to Candy's sister-in-law and said, "She deals with it this way." Her sister-in-law weighed over three hundred pounds and had created a wall of buffering fat, fuelled by food to protect her from her own husband's abusive, controlling nature. And then she pointed at Candy. "And you deal with it your way," alluding to Candy's anorexic body, clearly disappearing before everyone's sight. Taking another sip of tea, she calmly said, "This is our lot in life. Learn to make the best of it because, quite frankly, you don't have any other options."

Candy was horrified at the cold response. Her mother-in-law's statement that Candy had no options mirrored the exact words that Candy's husband had voiced to her weeks ago. It was at that moment that Candy decided that she would divorce. Putting on a happy face, she waited until after the festivities of the Bar Mitzvah and the family had flown back to Perth before she told her husband that she was leaving the marriage.

To say that he was shocked was an understatement. Even though Candy had told him how unhappy she had been throughout their twenty-two-year marriage, he obviously had chosen to remain deaf to the way she felt and to her desires – after all, in his words, *she was married to the perfect man.*

In the weeks that followed her announcement, her husband insisted that the family get counselling; both together and separately. Candy did not see the point of any counselling, as she was leaving him not to work it out, but because she finally had had enough of sublimating and subjugating herself for twenty-six years. In the end, she was just fed up with all his self-centred bullshit. Yet, once again, she gave in and went along to counselling.

After seeing the therapist several times, in one of Candy's private sessions the therapist looked at her and said, "Quite frankly my dear, I don't know why *you* are here." Candy cried and said that she had wished that she had been physically abused so that people could see the evidence in scars and bruises.

The therapist replied that mental and emotional abuse is much worse because it is hidden. All one needed to do was look in Candy's eyes to see how damaged she had become after so many years of her defences being systematically controlled, bullied and broken down.

In those early weeks of their separation, her husband called Candy and told her that he wanted to meet with her that week to discuss something. Agreeing to meet at a local bar, his demeanour was bright and he said, rather excitedly, "This is great, meeting like this. In fact, now that we are divorcing we can meet once a week for drinks. We can have a Jerry Seinfeld and Elaine relationship. I can tell you who I am sleeping with and you can tell me who you are sleeping with."

Candy looked at him with horror and couldn't believe her ears. She replied, "If I don't want to be married to you, why would you think that I would want to meet with you or want to know who you are sleeping with?"

In the week after she left her husband, she found an apartment close to their home and began to try to piece a new life together for herself.

8

From Bad to Worse

Looking down from Heaven, Angel Ariel knew that Claire must move forward and make changes in order to grow, honour herself and to see herself as independent. She also knew that, to truly heal, she must take responsibility for her life and forgive herself and others in order to completely close doors on the past.

Had Claire given herself time to grieve and heal after her separation by nurturing and nourishing her soul, she would have drawn someone completely different to herself. Instead, by choosing to replay anger, sadness, blame and being a victim, the only possible outcome would be to attract someone similar in her reality. Angel Ariel watched as Claire was to be challenged like she had never been challenged before.

When R discovered that Candy had left her husband, he told her that his work as a builder had fallen off. He wasn't making enough to afford the rent on his unit and moving in to his parent's garage was his only option. Candy felt sorry for him and said that he could live with her for a while until his work situation improved. Within weeks, he had redecorated her apartment and updated and accessorised her wardrobe. Of course, this was all done with her money.

She was so proud to walk around with this gorgeous, younger

man on her arm. Candy's sculpted, anorexic frame and his years of champion bodybuilding made them quite the stunning couple and she loved the attention and looks from people. When Candy's friends asked her what he was like, she said, *"He's such a sensitive fellow; so good at decorating the apartment, putting my wardrobe together and ...."* hesitating for a moment, she blurted out, *"... you know, it feels like being on summer camp with your best gay friend."* Little did she know how prophetic her words would become.

Although R had been in a construction industry partnership with a childhood friend for fifteen years, he decided that once he moved in with Candy, he would not continue the business. He basically stopped working and lived off her. The stupid part was that she allowed it, because she had neither self-respect nor boundaries.

In the following week, Candy's husband insisted that she meet him at a café, where he asked her when she would end this foolishness and come home. She told him that she simply got tired of telling him for over twenty years that she wanted to be shown some consideration and that she was as important to him as his career. With little to no respect for her wishes and desires, she simply left to find someone who would make her emotional needs a priority.

It was shortly after this meeting that her husband sent her a list of requirements that she would still have to fulfil even though they were not living together. He stipulated, in typical lawyer fashion that she would still have to:

1. Take J to school and pick him up at the end of the day;
2. Once home, she had to help him do his homework, make him dinner, spend the evening with him and then put him to bed. After which, she could go home.

Having never been involved in any aspect of looking after his children, whether it was driving them to school, helping with their homework, making them dinners, taking them to their concerts, or attending school and extra-curricular activities, it must have been an awful shock to lose his full-time servant. By presenting her with his list of demands, he made it clear he was not going to have his well-ordered life altered by a divorce.

Complying with her husband's every word for twenty-six years, Candy found herself going back to her former apartment to fulfil his wishes. Every time she entered, she would be overcome by waves of nausea. Even though it was detrimental to her health, she continued for several weeks. It was at this time that she booked a follow-up session with her therapist. When she discovered what Candy was doing, she was horrified and told her that under no circumstances was she to return to that apartment. She also said that her husband would have to finally 'step-up' and become part of his children's lives; now nineteen and thirteen years old. The therapist said that, in some strange way, Candy was giving his children back to him so that he could finally be involved in their lives.

When Candy explained to him that, under strict advisement from her therapist, she would no longer be following his requirements, her husband's face began to contort angrily and his words spat out at her like venom. "If you leave this marriage, I will destroy you and see that you are so ruined that you will be living in a tract home on the outskirts of town and your children will be embarrassed to ever come and visit you."

The seething rage under his threatening words cut through her and she feared for her life. It was then that Candy decided that, no matter how hard she tried, she would never be able to forge a new life for herself in Melbourne, as she would always be under the dark shadow of her threatening ex-husband. Praying to God for guidance on where she should go, her answer came the very next day.

R informed Candy that he would be moving up north to the state of Queensland as he needed a change and he remembered how much he had loved living there several years ago. Candy did the almost unimaginable and moved away from her children to the Gold Coast in January 1999. Renting a house along the canals, she lived off of her maintenance and support from her husband. The amount of money would have been sufficient for one person, but it certainly was not enough for both her and R. Finances had gotten so desperate that at dusk they would go fishing along the canals, not for recreation but to feed themselves. In desperation, Candy told R that he would have to contribute or move out.

With his building licence and plastering tools, R reluctantly applied to a few places for work, but it was nearly impossible to be hired since he wasn't part of an established crew or company. Eventually he was hired to do plastering work for new home construction, but he would need an assistant to work alongside him. He tried to hire young men to help him, but they could make more money working retail and didn't have to do backbreaking work. So, he decided that he would use Candy as his assistant, and because she had no self-worth, she agreed.

The humid Queensland summers would often see temperatures climb well above 32 degrees celsius and sometimes close to 40 degrees celsius (90 degrees fahrenheit to over 100 degrees fahrenheit); working inside without air conditioning felt like being in an oven. To avoid the hottest part of the day, R and Candy would rise at the crack of dawn and put on old clothes. She would fix their lunches and a Thermos of coffee. Arriving at the new homes, they would set up the scaffolding, mix plaster and hang plasterboards together. The hardened plaster was caked under her once-carefully manicured fingernails and impossible to get out of her encrusted hair. After an exhausting day of climbing up and down the ladders, it was hardly worth the effort of cleaning herself thoroughly as she was only going to be immersed in the plaster again the following day.

After six weeks of this gruelling work, Candy had had enough. Out of desperation and for her own salvation, she decided to look for work elsewhere. Because R lost his assistant and he couldn't hang plaster alone, he refused to work. Candy thought that if she got a job, it would shame him into finding a job as well. It didn't. He decided to go on welfare instead. Disheartened and deeply saddened as to how her life had deteriorated after only five months, she decided to put her qualifications as a primary school teacher to use. Answering an ad for a position at a childcare centre, she was hired in June of 1999.

This would have been a wonderful situation except for one thing. With her energies being profoundly sad and filled with disheartened negativity, she drew the same energies into her reality. This particular childcare centre was in a depressed, low economic area and the majority of the children were from broken homes where abuse, and alcohol and drug use were quite common. Instead of teaching rosy-cheeked, happy students, her days were spent dealing with deeply disturbed children and their parents. Most of the time, it seemed like crowd control instead of nurturing young, eager minds. Every day, emotionally spent with huge bags under her eyes, Candy would drag herself home. She thought that when R saw her in this state, he would feel some compassion for her situation and would want to contribute financially. The school children's uncontrollable behaviours and the depressive environment became too much to endure and Candy left the childcare centre after only eight weeks. Leaving her job had absolutely no effect on R and he still refused to find work.

Feeling utterly hopeless, Candy was looking through the local paper one day and an ad seemed to scream at her from its pages. It read, *'Are you at a crossroad in your life and need hope and direction?? Call Cross Roads Counselling and start living today!'* Feeling an urge within, she called and made an appointment to see a career counsellor. Cross Roads Counselling was to become her salvation.

Driving to her appointment, Candy noticed that she was feeling better. The choice to finally be proactive and help herself lifted her spirits. Parking outside a house with a white picket fence, she walked up the flower-lined path and rang the doorbell. As the door opened, she was greeted by a tiny Yorkshire terrier sporting a pink bow in its hair. The dog was an exact replica of a tiny Yorkshire terrier named Cleo that Candy had owned when she was a teenager. Behind the tiny dog was an angelic-looking lady who introduced herself as Mary.

Stepping into Mary's house, Candy was impressed with the many vases of roses and the beautiful chintz pillows adorning the tasselled couches. With the delicate scent of rose perfume in the air, Candy felt like she had just stepped into an Impressionist painting. Setting down a tray prepared with beautiful rose-painted china teacups, Mary poured Candy a tea and noticed the tension in her new client. Offering her a biscuit, Mary compassionately encouraged Candy to open up to her. Candy felt so comfortable and safe that she shared her heartache and sadness with this lovely lady. By the end of their first session together, they had spoken about various ways to restore her self-esteem and self-worth and to become empowered. As Candy scheduled an appointment to return the following week, Mary gave her a homework assignment. She told her to look in the employment section of newspapers that weekend and cut out ads that caught her attention. She urged Candy not to limit herself on age, background or qualifications. For whatever reason, if the ad took her interest, she was to cut it out and bring it along.

Over the next week, Candy kept seeing ads for a retail clothing store that would soon be opening in a brand new, off-price shopping centre. Having shopped discount and off-price centres while living in the U.S., this ad kept catching her eye, as it was the first centre of its kind to ever open in Australia.

At her next appointment, when Candy presented the ads, Mary asked her to explain why these in particular had caught her attention. Without hesitation, Candy said that she already believed in the company and did not have to be sold on this lovely designer label as she and her daughter had worn its clothing for many years; she loved the ESPRIT clothing line. Mary brought it to Candy's attention that she was speaking with a great deal of passion and enthusiasm. She then helped Candy write a résumé and came up with ideas that would make her stand out from the other applicants. They took an 8"x10" photo of Candy in a T-shirt (deliberately one size too small) with the ESPRIT name boldly written in red across the front of her chest and then attached it to the front cover of the résumé. Mary then had it hand-couriered with a bunch of red balloons to the head office; red was the company's signature colour.

Angel Ariel smiled down from Heaven. Mary had indeed been the answer to Claire's pleading for God's help. Angel Ariel laughed at the miraculous ways that He chooses to send the answers to our prayers, often sending us Earth angels who help us to get out of the dark and find the light. Yet Angel Ariel knew that sometimes we have to allow ourselves to be so terribly beaten down and disheartened before we let go and open to receive God's grace into our lives. Even though Claire was not consciously awakened yet, Angel Ariel knew that with her love of roses and Yorkshire terriers, she would feel even more comfortable opening up to Mary. Giggling as to how clever she was to include these details, Angel Ariel gave herself a pat on the back.

Several weeks later, Candy received a call from ESPRIT inviting her to a group interview. Sitting amongst about twenty-five young women, Candy felt light-hearted, with a giddy anticipation that she had not felt for a very long time. The girls were divided into groups and asked to role-play; with one person being the seller and the others being the customers. Upon hearing this, Candy was relieved; for if there was one thing she excelled at, it was shopping. Combining her experience as a drama major with years of shopping, she put on such a convincing performance as both customer and seller that the interviewers applauded her afterwards and said that she was the most believable out of the group.

God and the angels definitely smiled on her as she received news that she had been chosen as one of the twelve new ESPRIT associates to be a part of the anchor team that would open this huge store three weeks before Christmas. It was months later that she learned that the twelve positions were chosen from over five thousand applicants.

December 1, 1999, saw Candy, along with the other employees, sitting on the floor of this massive store as they decorated it for the grand opening. While threading green and gold stars, Candy turned to the recruitment officer and asked, "Sue, why me?"

Sue smiled and said, "Why you what, Candy?"

"Why was I chosen for this job? I'm forty-two years old and all the other girls are in their teens. I haven't had clothing sales experience and they have all worked in retail before."

Putting down her fishing line, Sue looked at Candy and replied, "When I hire, I don't hire on age or experience. The energy and the enthusiasm that you brought to the interview were exceptional. You showed me that what you have over so many of the others is that you cared and that you have passion. If a person has passion, enthusiasm, will and determination, they will succeed; nothing else matters." That job was the lifeline that Candy needed to help her find the will to live again.

One year after she left her marriage, Candy's financial settlement came through from the divorce. Soon after, she excitedly began to look for a house to purchase. The one she favoured most was a townhouse two blocks from the ocean that was still under construction and nearly completed. Wishing to secure its purchase, she put a deposit of $4,000 on it. In the weeks that followed, R said that she should have a final look around to see if she could get more for her money and suggested she go look at rural property.

Angel Ariel looked on in disbelief. Why in Heaven's name should Claire listen to anything R had to say because of his lack of any financial contribution to their relationship? And as much as she wanted to help her, Angel Ariel knew that angels are not to interfere with free will.

Candy and R travelled forty minutes out of town and found two lovely properties. In her heart of hearts, Candy really wanted that cute little townhouse. Yet, because she ignored her intuition and instead listened to R, she ended up buying one of the rural properties. It was ten acres overlooking the Coomera River, of which four acres were cleared and the rest was forest. R had grand visions of buying a tractor and clearing and working the land. This should have been an immediate red flag to Candy as she had seen him do very little work since they had been together.

Instead of putting the majority of her settlement money into her new home, R thought it would be a great idea to also buy a business. In this way, they could work together and earn themselves an income. He had told her of his experience working in his parents' fish & chips and pizza shops and decided that they should buy a café.

While she worked full time at ESPRIT, he scouted for businesses. R would occasionally meet her on her lunch break and he was always dressed impeccably, telling her that he had met with business brokers to help him find a business. That is pretty much how things went from September 1999 through until July 2000, when R found a newly established coffee shop in a prestigious shopping centre in Runaway Bay on the Gold Coast. The owners of the café saw their business as a small investment and wanted to offload it quickly after only ten months. This would provide them with the capital to purchase a much larger café in a trendy inner city district of Brisbane. Negotiating the deal, R used Candy's money to purchase the café and they opened for business in September 2000. Although Candy had a good job and was well-respected at ESPRIT, attaining the number one sales position, R explained that she should come and work at the café so they wouldn't have to pay another wage. Because she had so little confidence in her own decisions and listened to everyone else, it was with a heavy heart that she left her wonderful job.

From the start, R established that since Candy was an early riser, she should be the one to open up the café each morning at 8 a.m. Then around 1 p.m., he would come in for the lunch and the afternoon trade, and then she could leave. This may have been a good idea in theory, but it must be remembered that R didn't demonstrate the best example of work ethics. When he came in, there would be very little working on his part, as he would sit with the customers, drinking endless long black coffees and play the part of *Padrone,* or 'owner'. This was pretty much the scenario for the first six months. In fact, it was around the six-month mark that he decided he would only come to work Thursday nights and Sundays, with one other staff member. Still being the good girl, Candy allowed him this luxury and she continued working six days a week.

In those three years that they owned the café, she worked harder than she ever had in her entire life. Waiting on customers, clearing tables, washing dishes, preparing foods and taking orders, she worked right alongside her staff and lived on black coffee and cigarettes. Gaunt and exhausted, her weight dropped below one hundred pounds. Working the café was not only physically demanding, but she did nothing to nurture her soul and kept expecting R to emotionally nourish her. Not only did this not happen, but things really started to rapidly go downhill in their relationship.

Shortly after moving into her country house, R said that he had trouble sleeping. Blaming the years of working late nights in his family's restaurants, he watched TV until the wee hours of the morning. Knowing that Candy had to get up early and go to work, he told her that he would sleep in their second bedroom so he wouldn't wake her when he came to bed. Although she didn't like this, she thought it was somewhat considerate, until shortly after when she became aware of noises during the night. She would wake up to the sound of the front door closing and then heard the car starting up and would watch as it crept slowly down the gravel driveway without its headlights on. When she questioned R the next day, he said that he went on 'night drives' to get cigarettes. He said that driving at night helped him think and that he felt claustrophobic in the house. After a while, these drives became a nightly occurrence.

In addition to his strange forays into the night, every time his phone would ring, he would bolt out of the house and only answer it when he was outside. When Candy would question whom he was speaking with, he would remain silent. Once R moved into the second bedroom, not only did he become distant and uncommunicative but their sex life became non-existent. When she would approach him to discuss their relationship, he would stare blankly at her and turn and leave the house and her words were left dangling in the air. Totally worn out from shouldering so much of the workload at the café, and without any emotional support, she sank deeper and deeper into depression.

There were days when Candy would arrive early at the café, organise everything for the start of the day and go into the back room and collapse, weeping uncontrollably. Slowly she began to open up to her female staff and she felt supported by them. But instead of changing within by honouring herself enough to leave this horrible relationship, she tried desperately to change R. Screaming and crying how much she loved him seemed to fall on deaf ears, as he only became more defensive, silent, and unavailable.

Angel Ariel knew that the silencing of Claire's true desires and her deep sadness and negative feelings had created silence in her reality. The unresolved anger, sadness, bitterness, resentment and regret that she harboured for not only her ex-husband, but now R provided a constant internal chatter of blaming others for her life turning out so wrong. Even though the alarm bells in her life were so blatantly loud, Claire continued to be a victim and refused to initiate honourable changes in her life. Once again, Angel Ariel could foresee that the ongoing build-up of negative thoughts and unresolved emotions inside of her student would have to manifest as negativity in her reality. Yet even Angel Ariel could not have imagined the stream of horrible, negative events that were about to happen to Claire.

After moving onto the property, Candy was working in the garden and noticed that her balance was off. Concerned that it might be a problem with her inner ear, she went to a doctor. As he looked in her ear, he blurted out, "Oh shit!" Now, this is never a good sign under any circumstances, especially from a doctor. What he was able to see in the deep caverns of Candy's ear was a very large tick and, surrounding it, little baby ticks that had made a home in her ear canal. The insects were in so deep that he was unable to extract them and he told her to go immediately to the hospital emergency room.

Every second of her three-hour wait at the hospital was an eternity knowing that there was a tick family living in her ear. Finally when the doctors saw her, they inserted long, thin forceps into her ear and started pulling on the adult tick. The forceful tugging made her feel like her brain was going to explode. Once the ticks were taken out and examined, they told her how lucky she was that the insects had not been rabid.

Into their second year on the property, R not only continued to be silent, but he would disappear for long stretches of time with no warning or explanation. Being left at home alone so often, Candy decided to buy herself a Burmese kitten for companionship. She adored and bonded with her little friend, Simba, and they slept together at night. That is, until one morning Candy woke up and could not find the cat anywhere. Opening the back door, she screamed in horror as someone or something had disembowelled the cat, slit its throat and left it on the back door mat for her to discover.

Missing the company of her little friend, Candy decided to buy another Burmese kitten that she called Chloe. After what had happened to Simba, Candy decided to keep Chloe inside at all times. Going to bed one night, she snuggled with her dear little furry friend. The next morning, when she woke up, Chloe had completely disappeared and was never seen again. No one was in the house and all the doors and the windows had been checked and closed before she went to sleep the previous night. It was shortly after these incidents with the cats that their German shepherd, Loopy, was hit by a car and then shortly after was bitten by a rabid tick and had to be put down.

R resurfaced after being away, and Candy tearfully relayed what had happened to her pets. Unfazed and unaffected, as if he did not hear her, he said that he had returned only to pack as he was flying down to Melbourne for a few days to be at his best friend's birthday celebration. Again, Candy pleaded with him not to go because of all the horrible recent events.

During his absence, Candy came home from work one evening and noticed that the bedroom curtains were flapping on the outside of the house through the open window. She knew immediately that someone had broken in. Unsure if the intruders were still inside, she inched away from the house and drove to the neighbouring property.

Their neighbour, an older gentleman, accompanied her and they went into the house together. Not only had she been robbed of all her jewellery, the burglars had trashed the house. Immediately phoning R, Candy cried for him to return. He sounded detached and said that he couldn't possibly come back for another three days. Being unable to comprehend that he would choose to stay and celebrate rather than return to be with her, she waited three hours for the police to arrive, cleaned up the house and spent the night alone with a lump of wood by her bed in case the thieves came back.

On his return from Melbourne, R was uncharacteristically attentive and showed great concern for Candy. She thought that maybe the robbery had been a wake-up call for him to be more concerned about her. Yet, this was just his way of softening her up to comply with his upcoming scheme. (In later years, Candy suspected that it was R who had organised the robbery when he was away to give him an alibi. In this way, the burglary would be the catalyst to make her feel unsafe on the property alone.)

Having overseen every step that Claire had made, Angel Ariel shook her head. Claire needed to completely clear up all existing entanglements from this incarnation. And while R was indeed the needed catalyst to get her away from her abusive marriage, Angel Ariel saw R's true motives and she winced as she foresaw what was to happen next.

Slowly, his discussions started to centre on selling her rural property and moving closer to the coast, as he was suddenly worried about her safety in the country. In addition, he told her that rural property didn't increase in price as well as city properties and that he wanted *them* to get the most out of *their* investment. Candy was so emotionally neglected and physically exhausted that she could not see clearly what was so blatantly obvious to Angel Ariel.

This was the first time R had ever referred to her property as *theirs*. In later years, it would become clear that he wanted her to sell the property because it was in her name only. Then they would purchase another home together and, by doing so, it would allow him to legally share in her investment; just like the café. As it turned out, he wasn't concerned about her welfare in the slightest, but rather completely focused on his own future. Clouded by low self-worth and not taking charge of her life, Candy allowed this to happen.

In some ways, she was happy to move closer to the coast because there would be less maintenance on a smaller property and she would have a shorter commute to the café. She actually started to see it as a positive move, remembering the lovely unit that she originally wanted to buy, and was hopeful that she would be able to purchase a similar property. But in those two years, house prices had risen dramatically along the coast and the quieter neighbourhoods that she had been looking in before were now very popular and expensive. She looked at a number of smaller and older units that were actually more expensive than the new one on which she had lost her deposit.

Not long after, R said that he had to go to an auction, as there were a number of homes being released for sale. Candy said that she wasn't going to consent to bidding on anything that she had not seen. He said that they would drive past it on the way to the auction. Sitting in the car, two blocks back from the water, Candy sat silently as she looked at an old 1960s stilt home. The bottom floor of the home had been enclosed with fibro and, even with dusk approaching and the light dimming, she could clearly see that the home was in very bad shape. Candy was horrified and said that she didn't want to buy it. R said that the block was such a great location, and he swore to her that he would either renovate it or knock it down and build them a new home. Again, with his track record and lack of effort with anything that resembled work, she should have run in the opposite direction. But, buoyed by the prospect of living in a brand new house two blocks from the water, she agreed to attend the auction. With all the blocks failing to get minimum bids, they were passed in. R approached the agents and put his name down on the chance that the owners would reconsider selling at a later date. And, as fate would have it, reconsider they did. And that is how Candy came to be living in a dilapidated home, which was unliveable in its present state.

Again Angel Ariel, unable to interfere with free will, looked on as the deed of sale was co-signed.

With R now owning an equal share in the house, he did not want to spend any money on it and said that they would work on it themselves. As the carpet was forty years old, Candy insisted they replace it. Together, they scraped and sanded the floors and painted downstairs. Nothing they did helped this house because it was still a dump. The leaking, rusted plumbing in one bathroom only added to the 'ambience' of her new home and the other bathroom was completely inoperable. But, to top it all off, it had termites and the largest cockroaches on the planet. They would literally crawl over her at night and she slept with a can of bug spray next to her bed.

Retelling this part of Candy's story is truly like describing an unspeakable nightmare. Seeing it through clear-eyed vision, one can't imagine anyone having so little self-respect that they would allow a situation like this to perpetuate. Having completely shut down her light, Candy's outside reality reflected exactly the same darkness within. Once he had wormed his way into owning half of both her business and home, R had not only become more defensive and unavailable, he had also started exhibiting some rather strange behaviour.

Her dishonouring life and her depressive, negative state had started to take a great physical toll on Candy. While at work, she began to experience shallow breathing and dizzy spells and decided to leave work early. Walking in to their dump of a house, she saw a lovely designer shopping bag on the kitchen counter. Looking inside the bag, she saw several articles of women's clothing. Taking out the garments, she discovered a frilly blouse and a patterned skirt. Besides the fact that the clothes were not what Candy would have chosen for herself, they were a size 12 and her anorexic frame was a size 4-6.

Coming down the stairs, R was visibly shocked to see her home early and looking at the contents of the shopping bag. He told her how he had spent the day in Brisbane and had gone into an expensive clothing store. Nervously, he said, "The men in there were really nice to me and invited me to come back and listen to their band."

When Candy enquired about the clothes, he hesitated and said that they were for her. Candy told him that she had never in her whole life worn a size 12 and that he knew she was a size 4-6.

Looking like he had been caught out, he said, "Oh, they gave me the wrong sizes for you." When she suggested that they go back together and return the clothes, he got very defensive and said, "Well, they don't allow returns." (It dawned on her much later, that perhaps he had bought these clothes for himself, and not for her.)

In a desperate attempt to get some answers, she began to see psychics to try to understand what was happening. Every one she saw immediately said to her, "Who around you is gay?" One of the clairvoyants told her that R was spending his time up in Brisbane with his gay friends, who were bad-mouthing her and urging him to leave the relationship. In September 2002, R completely stopped working at the café and said he needed a break. As he did very little work, Candy could not figure out what he needed a break from. Without telling her where he was going or for how long, he would simply disappear.

Dragging herself home each night after long days at the café, Candy would sit alone and cry. Every day, she tried to call his mobile phone and it would either ring out or be turned off. Suddenly, a month later, R returned and told Candy to move of their house. Of course, at forty-seven, and without any confidence, self-worth or emotional strength, she was devastated to be forced into considering life on her own. Even though that is exactly how she had been living for the past two years, she cried and pleaded with him, but he was devoid of any feeling towards her.

During the next three months, she heard from several friends that he was making quite a name for himself as he was spending a lot of time frequenting the gay nightclubs in the Fortitude Valley area of Brisbane. Being in complete denial and closing her eyes to the obvious, Candy turned her attention to the very busy upcoming Christmas season and her responsibilities as owner of the café. It was during this time that her health became even worse.

Her weight had dropped dangerously low, and she started to have heart palpitations and increased shortness of breath. Each day started off with searing headaches and cramps in her neck and shoulders. Smoking a pack of cigarettes every day, her once beautiful complexion had become dark grey and her eyes appeared as two vacant, hollow spheres. She no longer had any energy left, not even to pray to die.

9

Divine Intervention

*L*ooking down from Heaven at the once beautiful soul who had held
such high ideals for her first Earthly incarnation, Angel Ariel wept
and felt helpless. Wishing desperately to assist her beautiful student,
Angel Ariel's deep emotions began to manifest help, and she suddenly
found herself standing on the cool marble steps of the Hall of Akashic
Records.

No matter how many times she had visited the Hall, each time
its beauty was more breathtaking. The reflection of the sun on the
temple's smooth, white columns created a bright halo of light around
the flowered courtyard. The bright pinks and purples of the hanging
gardens of bougainvillea framed the towering temple and a majestic
waterfall spilled from the side of a nearby mountain into a sapphire
pool. The fine mist from the waterfall floated through the air and clung
to the wings of the faeries and the angels that were also enjoying the
beauty of the gardens.

She gazed at the rose garden with its carved benches and
meandering paths and sighed deeply, remembering how this garden
had provided her with so much healing, comfort and solace after
returning from some of her more difficult incarnations on Earth.

Ascending the marble steps, she entered the massive hall. As a
Spiritual Teacher in service to God, she would often consult the Akashic

Records, which housed the information on all of the incarnations of every soul. In guiding and teaching others about spiritual laws, Angel Ariel had spent many hours researching individuals' incarnations to determine the areas in which to best help them align with their Divine eternal natures. Yet, as she stood in the enormous Hall of Wisdom this time, she felt absolutely helpless to guide her dear Claire to find her way to reconnecting to her Divine light within.

This great longing in her heart manifested the Etheric Council; twelve wise sages who began to form out of the ethers. Their filmy, transparent apparitions hovered in mid-air as they positioned themselves around a semi-circular table. At first, Angel Ariel could only discern their glasses, being momentarily blinded by the immense light that was emanating from them. This extraordinary Divine, white light of shared wisdom lead to the Council being also known as 'The Great White Brotherhood'. Angel Ariel smiled as she thought the name strange, for there were women who also sat on the Council. As if in response to her thoughts, she heard a woman's voice. "I do not take umbrage at the title of the Brotherhood and I'm sure the other ladies on the Council are just as accepting as I am."

Lady Nada was the first of the twelve Ascended Masters to manifest completely. Looking upon her Divine expression brought tears to Angel Ariel's eyes. As the other Masters slowly took form, Angel Ariel saw that the Council of twelve included: Lady Nada, Mary Magdalene, Mother Mary, Lady Portia, Quan Yin and Saint Germaine. These were the wise, gentle feminine energies that provided the wisdom and strength of Divine empowerment. Balancing these feminine energies were the masculine energies of Hilarion, Kuthumi, Buddha, Djwhal Khul, Serapis Bay and Lord Sananda. In truth, each one of these Masters is the perfect balance of both masculine and feminine energies. Angel Ariel was struck with admiration for each one of them, as they had incarnated many times back to Earth to help raise the consciousness and bring more light to the planet.

A hush came over the Council as Djwhal Khul slowly spoke. "Angel Ariel, it is our pleasure as always to be with you." Opening her

Book of Life, he scanned her many incarnations and her work. "Your work as an advisor and a Spiritual Teacher in Heaven is exemplary. Thousands of souls have had their faith restored and their light of God replenished due to your wise counsel." He paused a moment for reflection before continuing. "Yet, we have felt your pain and frustration as your student Claire on the Earth plane has continued on her path of self-destruction."

Holding back the tears, Angel Ariel said, "It is true, I feel helpless. What wise advice could you suggest for this beautiful lost soul?"

Conferring telepathically, the Council then spoke as one voice. "It is true that one cannot interfere with free will, but we have heard the cries and pleas from this frightened, lost soul as she has asked God repeatedly to stop her suffering and to end her life."

Angel Ariel sadly nodded as she had witnessed Claire's two failed suicide attempts over the past year. It was then that the Etheric Council said, "Angel Ariel, are you familiar with the term 'Walk-In'?"

She nodded, as she knew that a spiritually advanced soul would come to the higher self of a deeply depressed, often suicidal human in their dream state. Explaining to them that there is an alternative to wasting the body that they are in, they can willingly contract with another soul to take over their body and can then 'walk out', returning to Heaven with honours. Their body then provides a human vehicle for that advanced spiritual soul to come back to Earth as an adult to be of service to humanity.

As a Spiritual Teacher, Angel Ariel was aware that one of the greatest ways that souls learn their lessons when in human form is through struggles and hardships. By experiencing adversity, a person is often forced to make changes in order to grow spiritually. Yet when a soul on the Earth plane can't sustain their life force energy anymore and asks to die, she knew that there are certain exit points built into their contract to allow a human to leave their physical incarnation early. Although this provides a human with an alternative to suffering, she also realized that knowing something in theory and having practical experience are two vastly different things.

Ascended Master Kuthumi continued, "If you choose to be a Walk-In, you will be among many others who will be returning to Earth at this critical point in the planet's ascension. We are asking many enlightened beings who have transcended the karmic wheel of birth and death just like yourself to return to Earth one more time. With your return, you will hold your pure energy of love and light to help the planet ascend in consciousness. You would be doing the same work as you do in Heaven, yet as a Spiritual Teacher on Earth, you would be able to touch human souls with your wisdom and illumination."

Again, the voice changed to Ascended Master Hilarion. "With so many people beginning to shift, you would be able to offer spirituality and higher concepts to receptive, eager hearts and minds." Immediately, Hilarion's voice modulated into that of Serapis Bay. "You encompass a rare gift that marries not only the harnessing of the alchemical magic of metaphysics, but you also have the soft, imaginative soul of an artist. People are drawn to your gentle, welcoming nature and simply being in your presence helps others to resonate with a higher, more peaceful frequency."

The tone of the voice switched to a higher resonance as Lady Nada spoke. "If the planet is to ascend, then it will be through the rebirth of the Divine Feminine energies held hostage and quelled for too long. Allowing and encouraging these energies to return to the planet will provide the necessary mental and emotional healing after years of patriarchal dominance and control."

The voice then changed to that of Mary Magdalene. "Women must take their rightful place as equals to men, honored for their contributions and praised for their strengths."

The new voice of Lady Portia added, "By holding the balance of mercy and justice, this will restore the balance between hands and hearts."

With these words spoken, a hushed silence fell over the Hall, broken by two soothing voices as Mother Mary and Quan Yin spoke in unison. "My dear Angel Ariel, one of the greatest tools to heal the wounds of Earth is forgiveness for our treatment of others and ourselves."

The voice changed to a lower register as Lord Sananda spoke in a peaceful, compassionate tone. "You would help others to love their neighbor as they love themselves."

Buddha then continued, "You will have the opportunity to be the walking example of all these enlightened universal truths that will help lift the planet to ascension. As Lord Sananda experienced in his incarnation as Jesus, the road we travel back to duality in order to lift the vibrations of humankind is not without its challenges. Yet, the pledge of service to God, to bring about the Golden Age, is the most sacred and selfless of journeys." As Buddha completed his words, the Hall filled with a violet glow.

Rising to her feet, Saint Germaine spoke. "Angel Ariel, you would not be here if you had not already considered on some level to return to help the world ascend. Because of the accumulated dark energies that the planet has absorbed through thousands of years of bloodshed, corruption, judgment and hatred, Earth needs a tremendous amount of light to combat the darkness." After pausing for a moment, she added, "Angel Ariel, it is written in your Book of Life that you have the opportunity to be one of the many enlightened Masters who will contract to help shift the collective consciousness on planet Earth. In the guise of human form, you will carry out this mission from God, transmuting long held negativity into the radiance of love, peace and unity."

Hesitantly, Angel Ariel asked, "Would I be meeting with other Walk-Ins?"

It was Djwhal Khul who answered. "Each Walk-In will hold the frequencies of love and light for close to one million people. For this reason, it is imperative to spread them around the globe to balance the Earth's energies. In the majority of cases, when you are on the Earth plane, it is highly unlikely that you will be meeting other Walk-Ins. Beloved one, this mission requires an enormous amount of inner strength and fortitude that are the hallmarks of the Spiritual Warrior.

Most of the time, you will have only yourself and your profound devotion to God to support you." Pausing, he then emphasized, "Difficult tasks are not given out lightly by this Council, and if it is too much to ask for you to return to duality in the physical fields of matter, there will be no condemnation; as always the choice is yours."

The Council knew how difficult a decision this was for Angel Ariel, as she had vowed never to return to physical form. But they also knew that planet Earth desperately needed as many awakened people as possible to hold massive amounts of light to help it shift and ascend to a higher state of consciousness.

Feeling the heavy burden of holding the light, with very little support from other like-minded, awakened souls on Earth, she focused all her attention on her heart. She took a deep breath and sighed. "I have decided that I will return to physical form only if I can have but one request fulfilled."

Intrigued by her statement, The Elders leaned forward and asked her to state her request. "I will go back to the physical fields of matter only if I can be reunited with my Twin-Flame Kiel."

The Council then lowered their heads and began to consider and discuss the possibility of a Twin-Flame reunion on the Earth plane. The Elders knew that there was only one Twin-Flame, one Divine complement, to oneself in any space, time and dimension and that the reunion with a Twin-Flame on Earth was only possible when each person had cleared and completed all their karma. Unencumbered by this karma, they become a walking reflection of a deep, sacred connection to God within. It is this Divine reflection that becomes a magnet to draw the same energetic match of Divinity to himself or herself.

Suddenly, Angel Ariel became aware of the Council quietly waiting for her full attention. Lord Sananda rose and smiled. "It is unanimous that, even though the reunion of Twin-Flames on the Earth plane has been extremely rare, during your time as a Walk-In, you will be reunited only if your Twin-Flame Kiel agrees and clears his own karma. It is known that the combined energies of Twin-Flames, charged with Divine love, can bring even more light to a very dark planet. Twin-Flames like you and Kiel will be endowed with an exclusive, sacred mission from God to fulfil together before your incarnations come to an end."

Overjoyed at the possibility that Kiel might be with her in human form, Angel Ariel said, "I will start to visit Claire's higher self in her sleep-state this evening. And even though I will offer to help end her pain and suffering by agreeing to enter her physical form, it is completely and solely up to her whether she chooses for this to happen."

While The Etheric Council signed her final contract to reincarnate in human form, they added, "To help orientate you with the complexities of being a Walk-In, we will send you some help through a wise teacher." Closing her Book of Life, the Council spoke in unison. "Angel Ariel, we wish you well and our deepest prayers are always with you." With these words, the Council began to fade.

10

Lessons from an Unexpected Teacher

*A*s *Angel Ariel stepped out of the Hall into the bright sunlight, she decided to visit the comfort of the rose garden. Sitting on one of the carved benches, she closed her eyes and breathed in the fragrant scent of the blossoms. A voice suddenly popped out of thin air. "Well, dearie, when we go back, we can still have the joy of smelling roses; that is, if we stop to do so."*

Angel Ariel quickly opened her eyes and saw a grinning dwarf perched on the end of the bench. "Excuse me?" she questioned in a confused voice.

The dwarf added, "You know, the expression, 'Stop and smell the roses'." With that pronouncement, he jumped off the bench to his full height of three feet, took off his cap and bowed deeply. "Me name's Phineas and I'm walking in as well. I've come to take you to the orientation and give you some help. Follow me, missy."

With those words, he quickened his step, and in spite of his short stature, Angel Ariel found it quite difficult to keep up with his rapid pace. Walking to the end of the garden, they came to a thick grove of trees. Following Phineas through the dark woods, she became aware of a celestial chorus that filtered through the forest. Following the sound of these beautiful voices, Angel Ariel noticed that the trees began to thin out, as long shards of light pierced the darkness. Arriving at the end of the forest, the land fell away at their feet and in front of them was the City of Light. As far as the eye could see, in all directions lay a vast expanse of crystal and glass buildings. Their turrets glistened and sent rays of rainbow lights into the sky. Even though Angel Ariel had previously witnessed this magnificent sight, it still took her breath away.

Tugging on Angel Ariel's sleeve, Phineas broke her reverie with a gruff tone. "Come on, sweetie, we don't want to be the last ones walking in to the meeting." By the time they had arrived at the amphitheater, many of the other eager souls were anxiously waiting for the meeting to begin. Scanning the tiers of seats, Angel Ariel noticed the great diversity in the beings that had contracted to go back to Earth. Angels sat beside leprechauns who sat beside intergalactic star beings who sat next to mermaids. Every color, race, culture and creed was represented and patiently waiting. Well, that is, except the faeries. Angel Ariel giggled as she watched them darting back and forth over the heads of the audience, desperately trying to eavesdrop and pick up snippets of conversations. It was sometimes rumored that the faeries were known to be hopeless gossips.

Breaking her attention away from the faeries, Angel Ariel noticed an indigo light beginning to glow on the stage. As the light grew brighter, a strong, yet gentle voice began to fill the amphitheater. Stepping out of the blue light was Archangel Michael.

"Welcome and bless you all for agreeing to take part in the ascension of planet Earth. Mother Gaia is at a critical point in her awakening with many of its inhabitants choosing to consciously live in love, acceptance and unity. Without increased light, she will continue to succumb to the dark forces of hatred, racism, wars, corruption and greed. I sense the great wave of enthusiasm and anticipation from you Spiritual Warriors, as each one of you is on the verge of beginning this immense undertaking. It may be hard for you to believe that some of the beings that were chosen to return for this all-important mission declined. They did not want to experience enormous challenges while trying to find love in the contrast of duality. Yet, there were many

others who wanted to go back to Earth, but they were not chosen. They had not yet acquired the advanced spiritual knowledge, fortitude and inner strength to undertake and complete such an important mission." Pausing, Archangel Michael lovingly gazed at the audience. "Each one of you will hold a tremendous amount of pure, Divine love and every place you walk, and the people you come into contact with, will have their energies positively charged and raised."

Scanning the theatre filled with bright, eager faces, Archangel Michael continued. "I speak for all the Angelic Realm when I tell you how much pride and admiration that we have for you all. That each of you has made the decision to return to love, despite the knowledge that, as humans, you will experience fear, anger, loss and the feeling of separation and being alone in your various incarnations, is a true mark of your spiritual mastery.

"In conclusion, I need to tell you that, although you have all experienced incarnating on Earth before, this will be the most difficult. It will be more challenging than you can imagine because you will remember where you have come from and what you have come back to accomplish. Knowing your Divine connection, and recalling the pure love and acceptance you felt in Heaven, while trying to function on a planet where only a small percentage of the population is awakened to love and acceptance, will test your faith enormously. Know that you are more adored, admired and cherished for the great journey you now embark upon. God bless you all."

With those words, the indigo light began to fade from the stage. As if the dissolving of the color was a cue to start their journey, Phineas turned to Angel Ariel and said, "I will be your guide to prepare you for your experience as a Walk-In."

Weaving their way out of the crowded amphitheater, Angel Ariel said in a confused tone, "But aren't you also going back as a Walk-In?"

Trying to distance himself from the crowds, Phineas stopped at the edge of the forest and said, "Yes, yes, my dear, I am walking in too. But the difference is, I have done this before. I'll explain further, but first, come along into the forest. I feel so much more comfortable there."

As they meandered into the woods, the density of the forest grew thicker. The sparkling rays of sunshine struggled through the heavily veiled treetops. A carpet of dark moss covered the ground and a deep, lush scent filled the air. Angel Ariel noticed the nymphs and pixies darting among the plants and felt the wonderful energies of nature. Suddenly she realized that her foot was wet. Looking down, Phineas burst into laughter, "Don't you watch where you're going?" Having been distracted by the Elementals*, Angel Ariel had not seen the stream blocking their path. Shaking his head, Phineas mumbled, "I don't know how you angels survive with your heads always in the clouds."

Staring intently at the middle of the stream, a footbridge suddenly appeared. Stepping assuredly onto the bridge, Phineas noticed Angel Ariel's hesitancy. "Come on, lassie, don't you trust me handiwork?"

Gingerly stepping forward, Angel Ariel found herself directly opposite two enormous trees that had intertwined and grown into one another. At the intersection of the trees, she noticed a small door at the base where the trees had grown together.

Taking a large brass key from the pocket of his waistcoat, Phineas opened the door. Licking his lips, he said, "You know, walking always gives me quite a thirst. What do you say to a spot of licorice root tea?"

Watching Phineas easily fit through the small door, Angel Ariel hesitantly replied, "Yeah, sure." Just as she expected, following the dwarf's three-foot frame through the door posed quite a problem. She had to fold her wings very close to her contorted body as she wiggled in through the tiny opening. Squeezing herself into a little chair, she looked around at Phineas' cozy home beneath the ground.

Preparing a warmed teapot and a plate of blueberries, Phineas poured two cups. "Right, young lady, tell me all you know about Walk-Ins."

Taking a long sip of the hot, sweet tea, Angel Ariel took some blueberries and popped them into her mouth. "The first time I was on the Earth plane was during the time of Atlantis. I had come with others directly from the Angelic Realm to populate Lemuria. I was part of an alliance of inter-dimensional beings that incarnated to planet Earth. We came together in peace in order to create an astounding civilization." Thinking about her Lemurian life, she smiled. "Our brilliant technological advancements, powers of instant manifestation and harvesting natural energies through crystals were extraordinary." Staring off into the distance, Angel Ariel sighed and said in a dreamy, far-off tone, "It was a magical time of harmony and peace."

Phineas started to fidget in his chair as if he had a burr caught in his shorts. "Come on, girlie, pay attention! Now tell me, what do you know about Walk-Ins?!"

Angel Ariel said with assurance, "Well, the one thing that I do know is that I won't be incarnating as a baby."

Lighting up the tobacco in his pipe, Phineas inhaled the smoke and blew a series of smoke rings. "Okay, now that's a good start. You see the purpose of all incarnations into human form is to come back and learn lessons through the duality of contrast and challenges. I guess the reasoning is that, if a lesson came easily, we would not give it any thought or notice. When we are standing before the Etheric Council and writing our contract for our next life, we get to choose the souls from our soul group that we want to be our parents, siblings, friends and even our enemies. Depending on what lessons we want to learn, we choose people's characteristics that will test us and, in many cases, force us to grow."

Impatiently, Angel Ariel blurted out, "Yes, yes, I know all of that, but if we are to inhabit physical form without incarnating as babies, how does that happen?"

Taking a long, slow puff on his pipe, Phineas said, "Don't rush me, dearie, I was just getting to that. You see, there are many humans on the Earth plane who are so profoundly saddened that they can no longer keep their life force energy going and they wish to exit their contracts early and leave. Heaven's guides, like you, keep close contact with all humans and can clearly see when someone's beautiful light within starts to fade because of their despair. If this happens over a prolonged period of time, a spiritually advanced soul will come to the human when they are in a sleep state. They will explain to them that they can be released from their ongoing nightmare that they are living and return to Heaven with full honors by allowing a soul to walk in and inhabit their physical form. When this happens, the Earth person's soul, the Walk-Out, returns to Heaven, having given their body over to house a new soul."

Quizzically, Angel Ariel said, "But what if the former soul refuses to leave the body?"

Frustrated, Phineas began to wildly shake his beard. "No, no, no, my lass! This is not a tug-o-war over the body! Both souls must be one hundred percent in agreement in order for a Walk-In to occur. Believe me, the soul in the body does not take this suggestion lightly, for they are in such a perpetual state of despair that their higher self has asked God to stop all the pain and suffering. And it may take them many years of this experience before they choose to walk out – if that in fact is their choice.

"But when they both agree upon it, they begin to decide on an intersection episode as to when it will occur. Sometimes the soul walks in during a surgery, after an accident, during sleep or even a deep meditation."

Angel Ariel quickly replied, "That must be so exciting to get into a body and start getting things accomplished."

Finishing a mouthful of blueberries, Phineas said, "Well, it is not so easy coming from a higher dimensional frequency into a lower energetic dimension, such as Earth. I remember the first time I walked in on the Earth plane. I was quite dazed and confused and it took me quite some time to adjust to living in and around negative energies. And another thing, lassie, it takes a long time to get used to not having the powers of instant manifestation as we experience in Heaven."

Angel Ariel hesitantly replied, "Okay, once a Walk-In adjusts, then how do they proceed to accomplish their mission of raising the energies of the planet? I'm really afraid that I may not be able to complete my mission."

A scratching at the window interrupted Phineas' train of thought as he saw a squirrel peering through the window. Laughing out loud, Phineas said, "My friend is reminding me to enjoy the outdoors. Come, we will continue outside."

Stepping out of his cozy home, Phineas tipped his pointed hat to his furry friend. "The squirrel wants to remind you to honor your future and ready yourself for change by releasing all fear, worry and uncertainty. By trusting that your Divine mission will unfold perfectly, you will manifest an easy journey and travel with an untroubled heart and mind. Once you travel light, carrying only wisdom and love, your heart will be free, knowing that all will be taken care of in the most Divine timing and the most Divine way. Once you apply this, all your fears concerning the future will disappear."

A butterfly landed on Angel Ariel's shoulder as a sign of her upcoming transformation back to the physical world.

Relighting his pipe, Phineas continued, "Now where was I? Oh, that's right, you mentioned about accomplishing your mission in order to bring more light to the planet. Well, before any of that happens, you must adjust to the new life you've taken over. Remember, Walk-Ins retain the full memory imprint of the former soul; as the former soul's brain is like a computer chip that you access. Therefore, you'll remember to feed the cat, pick the kids up from school, if in fact you have children, or to call Mom for her birthday. But one thing Walk-Ins do not retain is the negative emotional imprint of the former soul.

"Therefore, the Walk-In is able to have a clear mind and be very focused on solving seemingly insurmountable problems that the former soul could not resolve, as their negativity kept them in a state of despair and pain. Free from negative programming and beliefs, Walk-Ins clear up the former soul's life in order to positively fulfill their mission."

They walked in silence for a while as the faeries darted in and around the flowering plants. All of a sudden, a thought dawned on Angel Ariel. "Phineas, if we walk in fully awake, then won't we remember our true names? How does that work with the former soul already having their birth name?"

Phineas smiled. "It can be very confusing for Walk-Ins at first. Having full remembrance of where they came from and who they are, they may not resonate with the former soul's name and they may choose to change it."

Thinking about that for a while, another thought occurred to Angel Ariel. "But what effect does that have on their family and friends? And if the former soul is in such deep despair and we walk in and take over their life, wouldn't the people in their life also carry negative energies as a result of the Laws of Attraction?"

All Phineas could do was nod his head and smile knowingly, as he had experienced all of these things when he had previously walked in. "Most times the former soul was surrounded by those who held a great deal of darkness and dishonor, which reflected their own pain and suffering within. With Walk-Ins bringing in high frequencies of love, joy and peace, it will definitely go counter to almost everything that is part of the former soul's life. It is for this reason that many Walk-Ins choose to divorce or leave their partners and find more like-minded relationships."

With a big belly laugh, Phineas gave Angel Ariel a wink. "Following the Walk-In experience, it can be very disturbing to go to sleep with Alice one night and wake up next to her the following morning, as you energetically have nothing more in common than your bed covers. But this energetic disparity does not only show up in relationships, it also holds true for other aspects of the former soul's life, such as their career. Walk-Ins almost always change their jobs, as they have a burning desire to be of service to humanity and often go into the healing arts and teach spirituality in some manner. In fact, in many cases, the former soul may have spent a lifetime perplexed and unsure as to their true purpose in life." Grinning, the dwarf added, "You know, that's one thing for sure about a Walk-In, they are one hundred percent focused on bringing their message of love, unity and peace to the world through utilizing their gifts and talents."

As Angel Ariel silently took in all the information, she noticed that the density of the trees became thinner as more fields of flowers appeared. Recognizing the gardens surrounding the Hall of Akashic Records, she saw that they had walked full circle. Re-lighting his pipe, Phineas began to exhale smoke rings that interlocked with one another.

Suddenly, his voice took on a tone of caution. "I must warn you, Angel Ariel. Do not be surprised if your tastes, opinions and beliefs change overnight. This will be your constant challenge; balancing the memory imprint of the former soul's programming with your own personality, perceptions and attitudes. In fact, if you can accept that all will be different in your life, then you will make this special incarnation one of ease and grace."

Angel Ariel noticed that his energies were beginning to recede as he slowly faded away. With just his cap, face and beard visible, Phineas offered these last words: "Take care, Angel Ariel. God speed and I'll see you back here one day to compare notes after our next Earth lives." And he disappeared.

Standing alone, Angel Ariel remembered her mission. Cupping her hands to her mouth, she shouted out, "Phineas, please tell me, what is my mission and how am I to bring it forth?"

A gust of wind blew the smoke from his pipe towards her as it began to form her answer. "Don't worry, you will be shown your mission, you won't miss it!"

Returning to the Hall of Akashic Records, Angel Ariel saw a long line of souls waiting by the steps. Taking turns, each one was handed a roll of parchment. Joining the end of the line, she learned that each soul was being assigned to a human on the Earth plane to see whether they wanted to return to Heaven and be released from their contract.

After receiving her scroll, she sat down on one of the carved benches in the rose garden. As she removed the ribbon and unfurled the paper, it looked as if there was a small movie screen embedded into the page and right before her eyes, the story about a beautiful, young girl began to unfold.

This remarkable little girl had been born clairvoyant and was an open channel, constantly receiving higher information. Her introverted nature belied her depth of spiritual knowledge and others took her merely to be a quiet, passive dreamer. This could not have been further from the truth, as she was constantly focused on connecting with seeing people and other beings from across the veil, as she easily experienced other dimensional realities.

The family that she was born into neither understood nor recognized her gifts and talents enough to foster and encourage her psychic abilities. Being unable to shine her extraordinary light, she found herself withdrawing from life and lived in her own world. As she grew up, she always felt different, out of place and terribly alone. Angel Ariel was amazed to witness this physically beautiful, talented young girl hiding her feelings of low self-worth; suffering hopeless despair from being so different to everyone else.

These accumulated negative emotions weighed heavily on this lovely girl's spirit. So much so, that she entertained killing herself and ending her misery. Slowly, she shut herself off from her Divine eternal nature and became invisible to who she really was. Instead of listening to her own heart, she began listening only to what everyone else told her.

As Angel Ariel watched scenes from the young girl's life, she winced as she saw her continually give her power away by not speaking up for herself. Not honoring and acknowledging her desires, the girl languished in a self-imposed prison of doubt and self-loathing. Following social dictates and doing the 'right' thing, she entered into a profitable marriage. And although her husband came from a wealthy family, he was an emotionally and mentally abusive man. His controlling, heartless words and actions perpetuated her distorted idea of being unworthy. While watching the screen, Angel Ariel could read the young woman's mind.

Standing under the traditional canopy on her wedding day, she was going through a mental checklist that her programmed mind believed that she had to follow: her intended was rich, of the same religion, handsome and a lawyer. The beautiful girl grimaced for a moment, noting that love was not on her list. True, he was callous and arrogant toward the feelings of others, but she assured herself that she would soften him in time.

The scene quickly flipped several years forward to the birth of her beautiful daughter. By this time her husband was far too busy to concern himself with any aspect of the lives of his family, as he was totally consumed with climbing the ladder of success. Neglected physically and emotionally, the young mother gave the baby girl all her attention and love.

A wonderful son followed five years later. The emotional neglect and mental abuse she endured was carefully hidden under her guise of being the ideal, perfect wife. While effortlessly meeting expectations and tending to children, home and family, she continually blamed her 'shortcomings' on her husband's emotional distance.

Fast forwarding twenty-two years, Angel Ariel gasped as she saw a still-beautiful woman silently screaming out for her husband's attention. Her once healthy form had dwindled down to a gaunt, anorexic frame. Because she was neither seen nor heard by her husband, she spent hours every day in the gym, trying to reach physical perfection in order to be noticed.

Angel Ariel saw that the woman finally found the courage to divorce him. Yet she still clung to such low self-worth that she quickly drew to herself another controlling, abusive relationship. Her new love was a destructive, deceitful con man who took advantage of her sweet, giving nature and attached himself to her money and credit. Angel Ariel's heart hurt so much, as she watched this talented girl, living on black coffee and cigarettes, continually allowing herself to be disempowered. With her weight hovering around one hundred pounds, people became alarmed at her skeletal frame that carried a shroud of darkness upon it. Her breath was labored and heavy like a fish out of water.

As the holographic image of Claire's life ended on the parchment, Angel Ariel sobbed uncontrollably. Wiping the tears from her eyes, she vowed to do everything in her power to help release this soul from its perpetual cycle of darkness and give her an opportunity to be released to the light. The rest was up to Claire.

---

*Elementals – different kinds of beings and spirits, which inhabit nature. These spirits are usually invisible to humans who do not possess the psychic ability of clairvoyance. Nature spirits usually abide in trees, rivers, plants, bogs, mountains and minerals. They attach themselves to and promote the growth of every natural thing and exist as the life force in all living things, and include gnomes, elves, brownies, pans, salamanders, sylphs, undines, mermaids, water spirits and many more.

11

A Waiting Game

*F*rom *that evening on, Angel Ariel visited Claire's higher self in her sleep state and explained that she could be released from the pain and suffering on Earth. If she had tried to speak with Claire's physical form rather than her higher self, Claire would not have been able to cut through the fog and the darkness of despair to comprehend what Angel Ariel was offering. Years of self-denial and profoundly depressed emotions would have certainly blocked any understanding for the possibility of this soul exchange to occur. Yet Claire's higher self remained clear and willing to hear about this alternative to her current life of anguish.*

Angel Ariel stressed to Claire that there would be no shame, embarrassment or dishonour in being unable to fulfill her contract. In fact, all souls are highly commended for their courage in choosing to live a human incarnation in the first place. Angel Ariel assured her that there would be no failure as there is no judgment in Heaven. With souls who have crossed over having the clear-eyed ability to see each incarnation solely as that person's expression of their physical journey, each life is blessed, no matter what decisions that soul has made.

These nightly visits by Angel Ariel to Claire's higher self continued over several years. Angel Ariel knew full well that, even after years of offering a soul the possibility of ending their suffering, there is a chance that the Earth soul would choose to remain in their human incarnation. With no guarantees and only a burning desire to help, Angel Ariel showed up and presented the information in a simple, loving and compassionate manner and waited, as she had all the time in the world.

In the years of vigilantly visiting Claire, Angel Ariel watched her beautiful student being torn and conflicted. She knew that she was being lied to, taken advantage of and having her money stolen. But because of her low self-worth, she chose to blame herself, even though R now constantly told her to move out of their house. From a higher perspective, Angel Ariel could see very clearly that Claire's experiences were the direct reflection of her inability to respect herself, choosing to stay in a toxic and destructive relationship.

She knew that Claire's programming and belief system of feeling unworthy and undeserving was so deeply engrained in her cellular makeup that it would require an enormous energy shift within her to transform and transmute her negativity. And as a Master Spiritual Teacher, Angel Ariel knew that the most powerful energy in the Universe to transmute and heal darkness is love.

12

Receiving the Grace of God

Throughout all of Candy's pain and ill treatment, her closest friend Val witnessed her emotional and physical decline and provided her with constant love and support. Knowing of her friend's ill health, Val made Candy a part of her big family. Constantly inviting her over for dinners, making her endless cups of strong English tea and offering sundry home-baked goods, she brightened her beloved friend's mood and tried to fatten up her anorexic body.

In December 2002, Val mentioned that a friend of hers had booked a masseuse to come over to her home and provide massage services to her friends. The enormous stress Candy was experiencing working long hours at the café, coupled with her profound sadness, created a lethal cocktail for her body. Her shoulders and neck were twisted into tight, hard knots, which lead to debilitating headaches. Constant consumption of headache tablets had been her only solution. As the medication had no long-term effect, she decided to take her friend up on her massage offer.

Upon hearing this, Angel Ariel was absolutely overjoyed. Little did Claire know that by doing something nurturing and nourishing for herself, her whole world was about to change.

Waiting in Val's friend's lounge room with a cup of tea, Candy immediately felt herself lighten. Taking a sip from the delicately painted rose teacup and hearing the bright chatter of the other women, it dawned on her as to how extraordinary it was to be actually doing something lovely for herself.

After about twenty minutes, Candy's attention was drawn to the hallway as she watched a tall, young woman seemingly float down the stairs. She did not realize it at the time, but this young maiden was part pixie, part faerie and part water nymph, cleverly disguised in human form. Her flowing, straight hair, pointed ears and impish face completed this Elemental picture.

Hearing her name called for her turn, Candy followed this lovely girl up the stairs and into a bedroom. Stripping off her clothes, she was prepared to be de-stressed. The young woman introduced herself as Mel and there was an immediate comfort in their connection as they found themselves chatting freely. At just nineteen years old, Mel's confidence and self-assured nature belied her tender, young age. Unbeknownst to Candy, Mel had come to show her the next direction that she would be taking in her life.

As Mel began to massage Candy, her hands paused intuitively in the middle of her back. In her soft, gentle voice, she enquired, "Do you do Reiki?"

Candy said, "No, I don't know what that is." Candy was unaware that the Universe had tried many times to send her signs for Reiki throughout the previous year. One clear sign was that one of her staff members was actually learning it and had tried to explain it to her. With the constant negativity and sadness screaming in her ears, she was distracted and really wasn't listening.

Candy knew that one of her regular customers, Diane, was a nurse, but she didn't know that she was also a clairvoyant and a Reiki Master. But Candy was not clear enough to take note of any of these Reiki references. Quite frankly, it wouldn't have mattered how many signs she drew to herself because she chose to focus on her past instead of living in the present moment; she remained blind to any signs that the Universe had tried to send her.

Continuing with the massage, Mel explained, "Reiki is going to become very important to you." Candy didn't realize that Mel was psychic and picked up intuitive messages, as well as being an excellent masseuse. While Candy was dressing after her massage, Mel explained that Reiki helps relieve stress, clears emotional blockages, re-balances and renews a sense of peace and wellbeing. On hearing this, Candy let out a huge sigh. "That's exactly what I need."

Mel handed her a business card. "I practice Reiki. Would you like to book a session?"

God and the angels work in mysterious ways. This was the lifeline that Candy had been unconsciously praying for in order to show her the way out of the hell that she had been living, and she booked a session with Mel the following week. Candy bid her friends goodbye and noticed that when she walked to her car, there was a skip in her step that hadn't been there for years.

The Reiki sessions with Mel were not only healing, they were deeply cathartic. They provided a loving, non-judgmental, sympathetic ear for Candy to finally unburden how emotionally destroyed she had become. Candy wept uncontrollably as she recounted the deceitful, uncommunicative life of disrespect that she had been living. Each session was liberating and afterwards she felt more peaceful and so much lighter.

She enjoyed the sessions so much that she went back once a week for four weeks. It was during the fourth treatment that both ladies felt something quite different to what either of them had ever previously experienced. As Mel put her hands on Candy, the massage table began to shake and there was a huge build-up of energy as Mel's hands began to tremble. All of a sudden, it felt like a large bowling ball of electrical current thundered up through Candy's body. Starting at her toes, it travelled up the length of her body and burst out of the top of her head, lighting up the darkened room as if a distress flare had exploded.

Both women were visibly shaken and astounded by this strange occurrence. Afterwards they drank their tea in silence, trying to process what had just happened. This was obviously very new territory for Candy – and a new experience for Mel as well. Candy had had only four sessions with Mel yet, it was after this mysterious energy surge that she began to experience a deep yearning to meditate. Again, she had been sent clues about meditation for quite some time, but had failed to see them.

A lovely Sri Lankan man by the name of Tyrone had been coming to Candy's café for the past two years. Serene and calm in nature, he used to stop Candy as she rushed around taking care of customers. He commented that she was always so stressed and tired and he offered the suggestion that meditation might help restore peace and calm in her life. Candy laughed out loud and said that she was not about to shave her head, don orange robes and go sit in a cave, chant and eat rice. Tyrone tried to assure her that it was no more complicated than sitting quietly, closing her eyes and centering on the breath. For someone whose every second was haunted by internal voices screaming at her that she was a failure, Candy could not quiet her mind long enough to fall asleep, let alone to meditate. Graciously she declined his advice and ran off to fill orders. Yet, this one little encounter was enough to plant a seed within her.

Watching Claire's conversation with Tyrone, Angel Ariel knew that, in order for a seed to germinate, it must be given the proper conditions and nutrients to help it grow and flourish. And while she could not force Claire to meditate, she could send her messages and signs.

In the ensuing weeks, whenever Candy turned on the radio, she heard either a segment about meditation or an interview with someone who taught the practice. She overheard her customers talking about meditation classes and how much they enjoyed them. When she went to the bookstore, books about meditation would jump off the shelf. In addition, one of her regular customers invited her over to her home for a group meditation.

Slowly she felt drawn to take up the peaceful, calming practice that was so foreign to her agitated life. Going to a New Age bookshop, she poured over many books that would help her get started with this age-old discipline. Carrying a large shopping bag, Candy excitedly arrived home and ran upstairs to set up a meditation corner in her bedroom. (For the better part of the previous year, R had moved out of their bedroom and solely occupied the second bedroom on the rare occasions that he did come home.)

Taking advantage of her own private space, Candy decorated the room in pinks and purples and demonstrated one of the first signs of independence by locking her door at night. Holding the shopping bag, she gleefully upturned its contents onto the pink bedcover. Incense, candles, relaxation music, a meditation book and a very large purple pillow tumbled out. Arranging the pillow in a corner of the room, she positioned the candles and incense and popped the CD into a player.

As she lit the candles and the incense, she felt a shiver run up and down her spine. She was not awakened enough to realize that this was her higher self's confirmation that what she was doing was nourishing and honouring for her. Sitting cross-legged on the big cushion, she took a deep breath and made sure everything was done just right. This December 2002 had been a typical hot summer on the Gold Coast and the late afternoon sun streamed across her floor, as there were no blinds or curtains on the windows.

As soon as her eyes were closed, noisy thoughts and inner voices chattered in her mind, telling her how worthless she was and that she was a failure. Her meditation book told her to persist, as it might take a while to get past the 'monkey-mind chatter' in order to be able to fully relax. She recalled Tyrone's words and chose to concentrate only on her breath.

Trying again, she managed to keep her eyes closed for ten minutes. Even with the mind chatter, she felt a strange calmness that she had not experienced before. Suddenly she felt a lump arise in her throat as her eyes welled up with tears. It felt so wonderful to finally be doing something nurturing for her health. All her life, she had subjugated her needs and desires, fulfilling the needs of others to the detriment of her own joy. Blowing out the candles, she decided that she would definitely put aside special time to give to herself and make meditation a part of her weekly practice.

In the weeks that followed, her daily practice of meditation was really put to the test. Over the Christmas holidays, the café was bombarded with hordes of hungry shoppers. Preparing food and drinks for the constant rush of customers kept Candy and her staff working at a frenetic pace. The extended trading hours enforced by the shopping centre meant that the café had to stay open from 7 a.m. until late every night, including until midnight on several nights through the week.

Even when Christmas was over, there was still no relief in sight as the holidays on the beautiful Gold Coast of Queensland, Australia, signifies the start of the busiest tourist season. After New Year's Day, it seemed that even more people needed to be processed. She used the word 'processed' and not 'waited on' because her actions had become robotic and devoid of feeling. Having to deal with the endless crowds and long lines of customers, her emotionally raw nerves made her appear to be stretched thin; she became vacant and distant, as if she was already preparing to vacate her life.

At this busiest time of year, R was nowhere to be seen. Each day, she knew that she would be coming home to a dark, empty, termite- and cockroach-infested home. Looking back, the thing that really saved her sanity was meditating, as she had now grown to love the calming practice. As so much of her life was seemingly out of her control, she now looked forward to this beautiful, predictable ritual.

Shortly after the New Year of 2003, R once again resurfaced after a long absence and told her in a cold, unfeeling tone that she had to move out of their home. Deeply hurt, Candy had no strength left and felt an overwhelming panic. Full of fear and not knowing where to go, she felt paralysed. With no desire to live anymore, she asked, begged and pleaded to God to show her a way out of her misery.

Saturday, January 11, 2003, saw the café exploding with endless lines of people. With the post-Christmas sales and the height of the summer tourist season, Candy and her staff served the constant crush of hungry and thirsty customers and as usual, R was nowhere in sight. Finally, as the stores were closing and her last customer left, Candy watched as one of her staff members pulled down the shutters for the evening. As they handed her the keys, they asked what she was going to do that night. Knowing that she would be on her own once again, Candy felt an overwhelming surge of sadness as a shudder went through her emaciated body. She said that she was looking forward to a quiet evening, watching a movie and having an early bedtime. Dragging her wafer-thin body into the car, she had intended to stop for food, but she found herself much too exhausted even to eat.

Arriving home with a heavy heart, she opened the door of their 'dump,' walked up the stairs, and entered the safe haven of her bedroom. At 6 p.m., the late afternoon summer sun was streaming through the uncovered windows, bathing the room with golden rays that would continue to shine well past 8 p.m. Her cozy meditation corner seemed to wink at her to hurry up, come and settle into the big, soft, purple cushion. Although she had always put on some soothing music, for some reason she broke with tradition and decided to meditate in silence.

Lighting new, long tapered candles and incense, Candy closed her eyes and took a few deep breaths, trying to exhale the cares of the day and the crushing heaviness of the weight on her chest. Yet, unlike her previous sessions, she felt an invisible blanket of comfort immediately envelop her, as she easily fell into a deep state of relaxation.

13

Stepping from the Dark into the Light

Feeling deeply sedated, my eyelids were so heavy that when I tried to open them, it seemed like they had been glued shut. Once I managed to pry my eyes open, I was surprised to find that I was sitting in a dark room with the light of the moon streaming through the window. My usual meditation practice would have added only fifteen to twenty minutes to my 6 p.m. start time. Yet I was completely baffled that there was no more sunlight. Not only were the tall, tapered candles extinguished, but it was strange that they had completely burned down in only twenty minutes.

As I glanced over at the bedside clock, I gasped as the glowing time read 11:11. Utterly confused, I did not know what had happened nor where the last five hours had gone. I remembered that I had to wake up early the following morning to open the café. Standing up, I felt light-headed and dizzy, unsure of my surroundings. Hurriedly getting into bed, I was relieved as sleep came upon me quickly and I was thankful that I didn't have to give any more thought to what had transpired that evening and the strange sensations that I was feeling.

As the alarm clock sounded the next morning, I opened my eyes, and was horrified to find myself living in an un-renovated, dilapidated 1960s stilt home riddled with cockroaches and termites. Knowing that I had to open the café, I rushed into the bathroom to shower. The old, leaking, broken exposed pipes, rusty stains and broken tiles repulsed me. In horror, I backed out the door and said out loud, "Who would live in such disgusting conditions?"

Deciding to forgo the shower, I opened the closet to get dressed. Utterly perplexed and confused at the contents, I said, "Whose clothes are these?" Hurriedly piecing something together, I entered the hallway and saw two enormous cockroaches taking a leisurely stroll. I was sure that I was still asleep and experiencing some sort of terrifying nightmare. The rotted timber floorboards creaked under my feet, as I gingerly stepped between the exposed, rusted nails and made my way down the stairs.

Turning my focus away from the plaster falling from the cracked walls, I became aware of the rumbling of my empty stomach. Opening up the fridge, I was appalled at the contents. Half-eaten McDonald's burgers, cold French fries, pizza and diet sodas were its only contents. As a thorough search failed to uncover anything of nutritional value, I decided that whatever was lurking in the refrigerator would not nourish my hungry cells and I chose to grab some fruit on the way to work.

Thankful to be exiting this house of horrors, I opened the front door and gasped; I was seeing colour for the first time. The vibrancy of the emerald green of the trees and the stunningly crisp, sapphire blue of the summer sky were so beautiful and intense that I began to weep. I would later liken the contrast of stepping from the dark energies of that house into daylight to that of Dorothy stepping from her dull, black-and-white world to the vibrant colours of Oz. The affect upon me was so great that I was rendered completely motionless. Weeping uncontrollably, I stood in awe at the magnificent sight of God's natural wonders.

What I didn't realize at the time was that Candy's memory imprint was looking through the new, clear-eyed perception of Angel Ariel who had walked in to her body and that Candy's soul had walked out during the meditation. With most of Candy's life perpetually seen through the eyes of anger, blame, sadness, bitterness, resentment and regret, she had been locked in the self-made prison of darkness. By choosing to torment herself over the past and worry about the future, her vision was continually focused on the dark, diverted from living in the light and the splendour of the present moment. Now, I found myself riveted on the present moment and conscious of the beauty of God's bountiful gifts of nature for the first time in close to fifty years; but I had not yet realized what had happened to me.

Driving the car out of the garage, I consciously deviated from my usual angry behaviour of tailgating, speeding and acts of road rage, and found myself peacefully meandering my way to work. Oblivious of my usual obsession with time, I decided to take the longer coast road as I marvelled at the magnificent scenery and arrived at work uncharacteristically relaxed and calm.

That day at the café, the staff mentioned that there was something different about me, as my usual harried and agitated demeanour was now quite peaceful. A number of customers also noted how happy and cheerful I was. Although I wasn't sure what I had experienced during my meditation, it became crystal clear that living in the dilapidated house and being connected to such a deceitful, insensitive, uncommunicative person was in no way honouring to me. In fact, this concept of 'honouring myself' suddenly became very important.

I had no idea where this feeling of empowerment and self-respect had come from after being paralysed in fear and reluctant to leave my miserable, destructive relationship with R. Yet, I immediately started to make inquiries about rental apartments and cheerfully started the process of moving out. This level of optimism and excitement was in such deep contrast to the continual feelings of dread and despair that had been my constant companions. There was a newfound sense of serenity and assuredness that everything was fine and that God would take care of all my needs. It was as if I were snuggled and enfolded in a blanket of God's love and protection and that all would be well.

The closeness and reverent connection to God that I felt was something that I had never experienced before, as I was not previously attached to anything religious and did not entertain the thought that I was even spiritual. I now simply saw myself as a faithful child and servant of God, and happy to be doing His will, not mine.

Armed with God's love, this was my armour and shield of protection that catapulted me into taking action. Yet, unlike so many who experience relationship breakdowns, there was absolutely no animosity nor rage. This jolt to make positive change was devoid of revenge and contained no sadness, anger, regret, resentment or bitterness. Enthusiastic and happily moving forward with my life, I found that I no longer entertained thoughts of trying to get R to do anything; I simply found that I did not think about him at all. My only concern now was respecting who I was and honouring what would be in my best interests. This was quite a novel concept after living the complete opposite way for forty-seven years.

Over the next twelve weeks, I had the clarity and focused determination to extricate myself from the business, the home and everything to do with my former life. Where only weeks before, I had been drowning in a sea of despair and suicidal thoughts, I now felt liberated, like a bird escaping from its cage.

Over those weeks following my 'out of the ordinary' meditation, and without realising it, I also began to distance myself from most of the people in my life. I may not have been able to verbalise it, but my higher self knew that the people around me were there because of the universal laws of attraction. Most of them were an exact reflection of the dark, negative and sad energies that I had previously perpetuated. Yet, when we are in despair, as in most Earth cases, God sends us angels in the guise of true friends to lift our spirits and bring us joy. In the end, I was basically left with only a few dear friends who loved me immensely and helped sustain me with nourishment, both emotional and physical.

By choosing to now view my future with optimism and emphasise the exciting possibilities ahead, I unknowingly started to increase the positive energies inside of me. They fired up my immune system and improved my overall state of health. By focusing on what I positively desired, instead of on what I didn't want, I began to draw similar positive energies to myself. Again, I had no idea what had happened to elicit this new behaviour and increased joy of living. All I knew was that, each time I made beneficial and honourable choices, extraordinary coincidences showed up which increased the ease and effortless flow of my life. In every moment, I was aware of the joy-filled energies all around me, where there had previously been nothing but darkness in my life. This lifting of all negativity off of my soul was possible because I intuitively started to practice the five important principles that every angel who is in service as a Spiritual Teacher in Heaven knows and teaches others:

1. Responsibility

I knew to take full responsibility for my life as every person, place and event that I had experienced in my reality was present because I had written it into my contract to help teach me important lessons. It did not matter whether I experienced joy, unconditional love, deceit, dishonour or abuse in a relationship, as I knew that whatever appeared in my reality was for my highest good and there to help me grow. With this deep knowing, I immediately let go of carrying around the debilitating negative energies of blame, fault-finding and perpetually seeing myself as a victim.

2. Forgiveness

Having taken responsibility for writing in my contract all the souls and their characteristics that I had encountered in my physical incarnation, I chose to forgive all of them. With the clear knowledge that they would not have been in my reality had I not chosen them and their exact characteristics, the releasing of forgiveness lifted a tremendous heaviness off of my soul and created space to experience untold peace and happiness.

3. Non-Judgment

Instead of constantly focusing my energies on judgment and blame that had crippled my ability to take charge of my life, I could now see the Divinity in each and every person and knew that they had free will as to the choices that they had made on their journey. Instead of condemning others, I blessed them for wherever they chose to be on their path of spiritual growth, as it had nothing to do with me. In this way, I unknowingly allowed myself to walk my journey as I see fit, and released another heavy burden.

4. Gratitude

I now chose to put my focus and attention on the infinite blessings that God lovingly bestowed upon me as I knew now that everything comes from God. My newly-found perception of being aware of the grace of God constantly working in my life was in deep contrast to my former obsession with being so dissatisfied with myself and my life. It was as if the clouds of illusion had parted and I could clearly feel that I was a child of God and abundance was my nature. Therefore, I would always have what I needed and be provided for by the greatest Source of all.

5. Unconditional Love

I now chose to love purely, openly, honestly and unconditionally as I could clearly see the Divinity in myself and others.

My staff and close friends were happy to see me beaming with joy, as they had seen the neglect and disregard I had endured from R, but they didn't realise for a minute that, under the same physical exterior, Angel Ariel had entered the body. In fact, in the beginning, neither did I. All recognition of who I really was had been temporarily halted as I had come from a higher dimensional reality into the dense, lower vibrations of Earth. Although I appeared the same physically, I was aware of the enormous changes in my attitudes and emotions that were propelling me forward into a much different, very new and positive life.

Choosing to live this way, I was now clear enough to hear the voice of God speaking through my heart. It was telling me very clearly to leave R, the termites, the cockroaches and the hell home, and to find a new place to live. Being a faithful child of God, I started to joyfully pack to start my new life. Surrounded by bubble wrap, cartons and packing tape, it suddenly dawned on me that I had no money, as my lovely partner had syphoned it all from our shared business, which I had financed.

And even though R had demanded that I vacate the house in the next three weeks, I felt remarkably calm, as if a blanket of peace were enfolding me, and I knew that everything would work out perfectly. Turning my attention back to the packing, I received a strong image of my ex-husband, along with an emphatic, intuitive message to pen a letter of gratitude and appreciation to him.

It had been four years since our divorce and there were no signs as to when he would release the final payment of my financial settlement. Having allowed him to draw up the agreement for the divorce, he had full control over when the last of the payments would ever occur.

Heeding the message, I then sat down and composed a letter to him. I stated that I felt that it was about time that I told him how grateful and appreciative I was for the life of wealth and beautiful opportunities that his hard work had afforded me and our children. I thanked him for the beautiful homes in which we lived, the children's private school tuitions that we could so easily afford, the wonderful international trips that we were able to take, and the many forms of entertainment of which we were privileged to take advantage.

I thanked him for his dedication to his work, and the sacrifices that he made in order to provide for us, and stressed how grateful I was for his efforts. I did not write one word about his controlling behavior and emotional and mental abuse.

Before I sent the letter, I quietly called in my higher self and I also called in my ex's higher self. I acknowledged that I had written him into the contract of my life to help me learn my lessons. I thanked him for loving me so much that he had given up part of his incarnation in order to play a contrasting role in the theatre of my life, so that I would really honor myself. I blessed him for exactly where he chose to be on his path and then I released him from having any negative effect on my life.

Holding the letter lovingly in my hands, I closed my eyes and saw my ex's face before me. I then called in the angels to hold him in their love and healing energies. I lovingly sent and surrounded his heart in emerald green, healing light and the pink colour of unconditional love. Posting the letter with just this intention of sending him love, I continued every day to send him prayers of healing, comfort and forgiveness.

A week later and a few weeks before I was told to move out of the house, I received an out-of-the-blue call from my ex's attorney. In a rather dry, emotionless way, his lawyer informed me that the last payment of my financial settlement would be deposited into my bank account that afternoon. God, in all His glory, had orchestrated that this money be held back for three years for the greatest good of all. If the money had been released prior to the Walk-In experience, then the former soul would have allowed R to get his hands on that money as well and drain it away, as had happened to Candy's previous funds.

It was as if Heaven were continually smiling down on me and orchestrating miracles to lead me down a very different and enchanted path.

14

Welcome Back to Earth, Angel Ariel

Knowing that something had to have happened to me, I began to frequent bookshops in search of information that might explain these drastic, transformative changes. While I was pouring over titles in the New Age section of one of these bookstores, I met the manager, Robyn, a diminutive faerie in a woman's body, with a larger-than-life personality.

As she assisted me while I searched the shelves, I explained to her what I had experienced and she tried to help me find some information. I did not know it at the time, but Robyn was very intuitive and saw visions. With our shared interest in spirituality, we quickly became very close friends, as close as sisters.

We met for coffee one day and Robyn told me that, even before we met, she knew immediately that there was something different about me when I walked into the bookshop. She explained that the first time she saw me enter the store, she watched in amazement, as there was a huge beam of white light over my head, following me. And although I felt fortunate and relieved to share my mysterious life changes with my new friend, neither of us could explain what had brought about this transformation. Seeking to offer some help, Robyn shared that she had heard about a renowned clairvoyant by the name of Patrick Moore who was working at a New Age shop called Tarot

Lodge in Surfers Paradise on the Gold Coast. The great news was that it was only fifteen minutes from where I lived. The not-so-good news was that, because of his international popularity, it was almost impossible to get an appointment with him. She said that if I could not get an appointment with Patrick, she had a friend, John Chamberlain, who could help me. John was a spiritual healer who had been working overseas with the psychic surgeons in the Philippines and had just returned that week. I immediately booked an appointment to see John the following day.

And even though Robyn had told me how difficult it was to secure a reading with Patrick, I felt a great urgency to call and make a booking; no matter how far in the future it was going to be. Calling Tarot Lodge, I explained that I had heard that Patrick was booked far in advance, but that I would like to make an appointment to see him. The gentleman on the phone laughed. "You must be the luckiest girl in the world. Right before you called, we had a cancellation. Can you be here in an hour?" As a shower of tingles coursed through my body, I said goodbye to Robyn and headed downtown.

As I walked into the store, a kind gentleman showed me to a back room. Opening a curtain, he announced to Patrick that his next client had arrived. Looking up from behind his desk, Patrick appeared astonished and his eyes became very large. He approached me, held out his hands and said, "Beloved lady, welcome back. You must be very confused." Gently taking my hands, as if leading a fragile, vulnerable child, he added, "It is so good to see you again. Here, let me make you a cup of tea and explain what has happened."

Without mentioning any of the enormous character changes that I had experienced over the previous twelve weeks, Patrick confirmed and explained exactly what had happened to me. His words sent shock waves and shivers of confirmation coursing throughout my body. Huge, grateful tears flowed freely down my cheeks as he expressed with great certainty, "Yes, my dear, it is obvious, you are an Angel incarnate from the Angelic Realm; you have had a Walk-In experience."

Explaining to me who I was and the reason why I had returned, he said, "Your mission that you have taken on is very grand indeed, and your service and message to humanity will be far-reaching." He looked down at the palms of his hands. "I am but a lowly dragon from the Dragon Realm, and my hands do not have much written on them. Yes, it is true, I do a good job bringing forth messages for people, as dragons do have a reputation for being helpful." Pausing for a moment, he laughed in a high-pitched tone, "Kind, gentle dragons like me, that is."

Picking up my hands and staring at my palms, he said, "But look at your hands; they have the mysteries and the teachings of the ages held within them, as you are here to impart and share your wisdom and knowledge with many." Breaking into a wide smile, he added, "Dragons and Angels are the best of friends, and I am sure that we have been reunited once again to be of service to one another."

At the end of the reading, we hugged each other tightly. I left the shop with an excited feeling in my heart, as valuable information had been revealed explaining what I had been through.

And even though I was elated that I had been given an explanation, I cautiously reflected on the information. Just because someone tells you something, even if he is an internationally renowned psychic, does not prove anything. Yet, it was uncanny how he confirmed what I had experienced for the previous three months without me uttering a single word.

Deciding to keep my appointment with Robyn's friend, John, the next day, I walked up the steps to his house and rang the doorbell. A very tall, older man with a head of bright white hair filled the doorway. As he ushered me into his healing room, he exclaimed, "Wow, look at the entourage of angels that is accompanying you." Pausing, his expression changed and his eyes grew large. "I am being told that this is your family and that you are one of them. Do you know that you are an Angel and that you are a Walk-In?"

15

Walk-Ins – A Whole New World

Just imagine that your whole life had been spent drowning in feelings of shame, low self-worth and of being unable to acknowledge whom you truly are. Imagine that every day you spent smothered under a soundproof blanket that silenced your words and covered you in a cloak of invisibility.

Imagine also, waking up one day from this endless nightmare and knowing with one hundred percent certainty that you are a perfect, Divine child of God and that you are more magnificent, beautiful and powerful than you ever believed. With the feeling of God's love and protection pervading every cell in your body, you start to slough off the accumulated negative emotions of anger, sadness, bitterness, regret and resentment and slowly start to replace them with joy, acceptance, unconditional love and gratitude for your infinite blessings.

Realising your Divine, inherent birthright that you are pure love, limitless and abundant, you re-ignite the beautiful light within that had been all but completely extinguished. With no more constriction, you start to breathe freely for the first time in your life.

This is what happened to me during a deep meditation on Saturday, January 11, 2003. I am a Walk-In. I come from the Angelic Realm and my name is Angel Ariel.

To better understand the complexity of what a Walk-In actually is, it is helpful to understand the similarities and characteristics that many of us share and demonstrate. A Walk-In experience occurs when a soul on the Earth plane becomes so deeply saddened and disillusioned by their human experience that they unconsciously ask to be released early from their earthly contract. In other words, they ask to die.

Every soul who incarnates in human form writes the contract of their life and chooses when they will exit their incarnation. In this way, they exit exactly when they have contracted to leave. This strong desire to end their physical life early may be a result of sustained mental and/or emotional depression, trauma and/or suicidal desires. In this case, the person is so exhausted by the continual abuse that they have endured that they simply want to exit in order to stop the pain and suffering.

A person may be so shut off on a conscious level that they never share their pain and torment with another living soul. Yet, their own soul, or higher self, is more than willing to seek help for them and bring more light into their lifeless existence. Since we are continually being protected, guided and watched over by angels and spirit guides, these non-physical guardians constantly monitor how human beings are coping on Earth. Because they can't interfere with free will, sometimes they look on helplessly as some human beings slip further and further away from the light of Divine connection and they get lost in the darkness.

Those of us in a physical incarnation have all drawn varying degrees of hardship to ourselves in order to challenge us to grow spiritually. And in most cases, souls will be able to endure their hardships, find the strength to go beyond their suffering and reconnect with their light within. Hardships often lead us to becoming more empowered, as the experience of adversity strengthens our conviction in ourselves.

Yet, when the Earth soul has shown no inclination to gain control of or empower their lives, and continually asks to exit their contract early, an awakened, spiritually advanced soul will initiate a dialogue on an unconscious level with them, often in their dream state. In this conversation, they will present the possibility of the human soul giving up their incarnation with full permission in order for another soul to walk in and take over their physical body. This is a contract between two souls and not possession, as it is solely dependent on the free will of the human's higher self.

Now, the Walk-In isn't just anyone who wants to come back for another stroll around the planet. As a result of their advanced spiritual enlightenment, a Walk-In has earned the right to ask humans who are in deep pain if they would like to be released from their earthly contract. Walk-Ins have such an important role to play in raising the consciousness and energies of Earth that they can by-pass the usual process of entering a baby's body at birth. In this way, they don't have to wait to grow up but can immediately be effective in their service to humanity.

With spirit guides and guardian angels carefully monitoring human souls, they can clearly see the systematic shutting down of a person's Divine light within and hear their prayers to be released. Only then does an advanced spiritual soul begin to address the deeply saddened Earth soul in their sleep and their conversation may go something like this: *"Instead of committing suicide and wasting the body that you are in now, you can be of service to the Light and allow me to help you. In so doing, you can go home to God and Heaven with full honours and end your pain and suffering."* The Walk-In would make it very clear to the human soul that there is no shame nor failure in not having completed their contract.

In addition, the Walk-In explains that they will accept the full responsibility for the human soul's life. For instance, the Walk-In will contract to pay the bills, remember important birthdays, service the car, etc. The reason that everything will be followed precisely is because the Walk-In retains the complete memory imprint of the previous soul. Much like a computer chip, the former soul's brain retains every minute detail of the information that they experienced in their life.

But what they don't acquire is the deeply sad and tormented emotional imprint that goes along with the previous soul's life. In fact, the Walk-In brings a crystal clear ability to solve longstanding, often insurmountable emotional problems that were left behind by the former soul. This is tantamount for the Walk-In to be able to create a new life. If they were saddled with the same unresolved emotional sadness of the former soul, it would greatly hamper the Walk-In from doing their important work.

Usually, the souls will spend a lot of time discussing their possible exchange. This kind of thing doesn't just happen overnight and in some cases, it can take years. When both souls are in full agreement, an 'intersection episode' will be planned for the exchange to take place. Walk-Ins can occur as a result of a serious illness, during a surgery, an accident, a near-death experience or during sleep or meditation.

Once the exchange of souls is complete, the new soul wakes up in the physical form, and has absolutely no recollection of the Walk-In experience. (They do not come in with a handbook detailing what has happened to them!) The process is blocked because that is what happens when one comes from a higher dimensional reality where there is no measure of time, and then enters the denser aspects of the physical dimension. Although you can't remember what has happened to you, what you do know is that everything is different and it feels like you are living the wrong life.

Your family and friends sense that you are not acting like yourself and they tell you that there is something different about you. And even though Walk-Ins inherit the memory imprint of the former soul, they are instantly aware of a remarkable alteration in their attitudes, desires and personality.

Many Walk-Ins change or adopt new names. I immediately started referring to myself as Claire Candy. This was very strange, because for forty-seven years I did not like the name Claire and would actually tell others not to call me by that name. Yet with all my psychic abilities opening up again – the clairvoyance, the clairsentience, and the clairaudience – I now felt comfortable with and fully embraced the name Claire.

Many Walk-Ins will divorce or leave their partners. It is very disconcerting to go to bed with someone who the previous soul energetically drew to them, and wake up in a complete energetic disconnect; as you no longer resonate with the former soul's partner. And while the former Candy had such difficulty and struggled for years as to whether to leave her deceitful partner R, I was crystal clear that I had to remove myself from his destructive, negative energies.

As well as letting go of long-standing relationships, Walk-Ins often have a burning desire to foster a newfound passion to be of service and contribute to the betterment of humanity. Many Walk-Ins, with their spiritual knowledge, go into the Healing Arts and become Spiritual Teachers. Prior to the Walk-In experience, Candy was never certain as to what she would do when she grew up. Although she had a Diploma of Teaching and had taught for many years, as well as created numerous businesses, she always felt like she was doing these things in the meantime until she figured out her real life's purpose.

It was crystal clear to me now that I was here to be a Spiritual Teacher to help others awaken to their Divine essence, and offer them help to live lives of joy, peace and reconnection to their eternal nature. I may not have been sure how that was going to happen, but once again, I knew in my heart that God would show me the way.

My newfound empowerment, and assertive and self-assured manner were particularly remarkable, for Candy's life was spent being a victim and so greatly co-dependent that she couldn't make a decision on her own; she always needed others to tell her what to do. Besides dramatic changes that occurred in my tastes in food and fashion, I suddenly was drawn to all things that were Scottish, Irish and Celtic. The music, the accents and the culture evoked a comfortable memory as if it was part of who I was, and these memories brought tears to my eyes.

Another characteristic of some Walk-Ins is that they begin to appear younger. I substituted long-held, negative energies of debilitating sadness, regret and anger with the energies of love, acceptance and gratitude. With these changes my physical body began to react to the lighter, more joy-filled energies, and my physical appearance started to change. The wrinkles and deep pools of darkness under my eyes began to disappear. The age spots on my hands dissolved and the pallor of my skin glowed and began to lighten.

Since that night of meditation, I had developed an obsession with anything to do with angels. I began collecting books, statues, posters and angel music. I also noticed that white feathers magically appeared and followed me wherever I went. I learned later that white feathers are confirmation that angels are around you. I went through all of these changes in the twelve weeks following that meditation on January 11, 2003. It was only after I had experienced the characteristics that accompanied this life change that I was Divinely led to the people and information that explained my Walk-In experience. In this way, I didn't read about Walk-Ins first and then begin to exhibit or take on the characteristics. Never having heard the term 'Walk-In' before, I experienced the transformation first and then learned the term and their often shared characteristics three months later.

16

You Will Be Divinely Lead

With all the enormous changes that had happened since January 11, I spent each day experiencing the rebirth of my newfound joy while trying to bring my world into the heavenly alignment with how I was now feeling. This meant that much of my previous negativity had to be dismantled and changed to reflect my new, positive, optimistic energies. Knowing that the date that R had told me to move out of our house was fast approaching, I wondered where to go. As I took a few deep breaths, I heard a voice distinctly say, *"You will be Divinely lead."*

The following sunny, bright Sunday morning enticed me to buy the weekend newspaper, visit my favourite beachside café and look for a new place to live. Ordering my meal, I opened the paper and started to pour over the rental section. At the table next to me, a couple was busy looking over the rentals as well. I overheard the man mention that his friend, Michael, who worked as a real estate agent, had told him that there were some new townhouses about two blocks from the water.

Upon hearing the name Michael, I received a shower of tingles. Because I was living only in the present moment, I could easily pick up signs that the angels were sending me and I made a mental note of the real estate agent's name. After breakfast I wrote a list of all the rentals and then began the exhaustive search to check them out.

Starting off with about a dozen places, I got more and more frustrated as the day wore on. All the homes were too old, too small or too expensive and my patience was wearing thin. At 3 p.m., I decided I had had enough and called it quits. I drove along the coast road hoping that the beautiful scenery would take my mind off of my disappointment. All of a sudden, I clearly heard the words 'turn left,' and because I had become so used to actioning my intuition, I immediately turned.

I noticed a large For Sale sign in front of a townhouse. Even though I was not in the market to buy a home, I felt an urge to investigate further and called the number on the sign. A man with an American accent answered the phone and told me his name was Michael. I instantly received shivers and remembered the conversation I had heard at breakfast. I asked to make a time to see the inside of the home and he said that he could come over right away.

Hanging up, I clearly saw a vision of a Native American. Within five minutes, a car drove up, parked across the street and a large, handsome man stepped out of the car. He introduced himself and we felt an instant connection as Americans living overseas. We chatted as I looked at the townhouse and he mentioned that he was an ex-army man and played football. He told me that he was from the Midwest and that his family was descended from a Native American tribe. We were so engrossed in finding out about each other that the townhouse had become secondary.

Walking on to the footpath, he mentioned that he didn't have any other appointments for the rest of the day and wondered if I would like to continue the conversation over drinks. I was flattered and told him I would meet him at a local spot. It was late in the afternoon and the ease and flow of our laughter and conversation took the hour way past sunset and we decided to go out for dinner.

Mixing business with pleasure, he asked me what kind of house I was looking to purchase. I explained to him that I was actually looking to rent a place, initially on a short-term basis as I was still trying to figure out the next direction in my life. He brightened as he told me that there were some lovely apartments across from the Broadwater in Southport along Marine Parade. Again, a series of shocks and shivers tingled through me and caught my attention. After a lovely dinner, we exchanged phone numbers and he said that he would call me the following week.

The next morning, I decided to check out Michael's suggestion of the apartment building across from the ocean. Walking into the beautifully decorated lobby, I waited for the receptionist, who was on the phone. I noticed the light, inviting energies and loved the flowing fountains and the flowered gardens in the front.

After the receptionist finished her call, I enquired if there were any units for rent in the building. She looked surprised and told me that most of the apartments were owner-occupied and the few rentals in the building were all tenanted. Then she said, "However, that call that I was just on was with one of the owners who is going away for six months and wants us to rent his one bedroom, fully furnished apartment. Would you like to take a look at it?" I, of course, said yes and after a quick look, I signed a three-month lease and it was mine.

Having already packed my personal belongings, I moved out a few days later and left all the furniture behind. I decided that I wanted to start afresh and did not want to take items that were filled with so much negativity. After a long day of moving and organizing, I stood incredulous as I looked out across the stunning ocean view from my balcony. My new home was a tiny oasis of light and bright energies for me to rebuild my strength, focus on my joy and bring my life back to peace and harmony.

Preparing a hot bath, I eased into the water and allowed myself quiet reflection to review all that had transpired in such a short time to lift me out of hell and to now experience bliss. I was grateful for the soft, inviting bed and the chance to rest after so much had been revealed. Feeling an overwhelming rush of being loved, I began to cry, closed my eyes and drifted off to sleep.

In the middle of the night, I sensed a presence in my room and heard muffled voices. Slightly opening my eyes, I saw that it was dark outside but there was a soft, incandescent glow lighting the room from within. As I fully opened my eyes, I began to perceive through the glow that there were many tall beings of light squeezed into the room, staring down at me. They had human form and looked as if someone had stretched them up to seven, eight and nine feet tall. Upon seeing that I was awake, the intensity of the light that was coming off them increased. Instead of being afraid, I tuned into their tender energies and they lovingly assured me that they were here to protect and guide me. When I asked them who they were, they replied, "We are your angelic family, as you are one of us. We are to be known as 'The Posse of Angels' as we go before you, beside you, above and below you and always have your back."

As Michael had promised, I received a call from him the following week asking me out on another date. And even though the memory of our first date was lovely, our next date gave my intuition something to question. Inviting me to an expensive restaurant, when the waiter took our orders, he proceeded to ask for only a drink. He encouraged me to order but said he was not feeling well and didn't want to eat. He then asked me if I was a good cook. I said that I had been known to make a great pasta sauce. He said, "Maybe you can cook dinner for me some time," so I invited him over on Friday night.

Michael arrived with a bottle of wine and flowers. I prepared a beautiful dinner and afterwards he ended up staying the night. The strange part was that he was well prepared to spend the evening. Early the next morning, he went down to his car and brought up a full change of clothes and his toiletries. He changed to go to work at his real estate office, only five minutes away from my apartment, thanked me for the lovely night, and left.

Needless to say, he never took me out to a restaurant again. Within a short time, we had fallen into the routine of him coming over to my apartment after work, sitting in front of the TV with a beer, as I made him dinner. On the fourth night that I allowed this behaviour, I suggested we go out for dinner on Friday night. He said that, unfortunately, his mother was sick and that he would have to go to Brisbane to see her.

As synchronicity would have it, a new friend in my apartment complex invited me out with some of her girlfriends on that Friday night. During the evening, I saw Michael groping and getting very friendly with someone at the bar who looked far too young to be his mother. I called him the next day and told him that I was not interested in continuing our relationship any longer. Afterwards, I spent a great deal of time reviewing how to fully respect and honour myself by establishing boundaries.

Knowing full well that whatever is in our reality we bring to ourselves, I analysed the relationship with Michael. He was definitely a compromise as to what my heart truly desired. It was then that I realized that I had not told God exactly what I wanted in a loving relationship. In fact, in all my relationships, I had shown the Universe that I was prepared to put up with disrespectful behaviour and I never really addressed what qualities I wanted in a cherished partner. Having experienced a wake-up moment of clarity, I took out a piece of paper and decided to write a letter to God.

17

My Decree to God

As I stared at the blank sheet of paper, I declared out loud to God, *"I desire a worthy, beautiful relationship, and although I am prepared to make certain compromises, I will show you, God, that I will never again compromise my soul when it comes to love and what I most truly desire."* I then wrote:

> *"Dear God, Thank you for my soul mate relationship."*

I looked at this sentence and felt a great uneasiness as I focused on the term 'soul mate.' Equipped with my angel's ability and spiritual wisdom to now see things from a higher perspective, I knew that both of my exes had been my soul mates. A soul mate is someone who contracts to be part of your life to help you learn your lessons and clear your karma. In this way, they reflect back to us some of the issues that still need to be addressed within us. Many times soul mates come in with great contrasts along with agitation, irritation and great drama. By pushing our buttons in order to really get our attention, they challenge us to honour who we Divinely are. Knowing that, along with great love, soul mates can bring deep heartache and pain to a relationship, I quickly erased the words 'soul mate.' I then easily wrote:

> *"Dear God, Thank you for my Twin-Flame relationship."*

Again, as a Spiritual Teacher in service to the Divine, I knew that there exists only one Twin-Flame relationship for each one of us and it is not duplicated in any space, time and dimension. This is our Divine perfect complement and I knew that one does not find one's Twin-Flame by searching for them. By clearing and cleansing one's karma, one begins to emit the high-energy frequency of a Divine, pure love. It is this high frequency within the self-realised person that draws their exact vibrational match to themselves, if that Twin-Flame is on the Earth plane and if they have also cleared their karma. One can only attract this blissful, perfect complement when one attains the matching reflection of this blissful perfection inside of them. Looking at the start of my letter, I sensed that something else was missing. It was then that I added:

"...and marriage."

Having experienced many past lives in which traditions were followed, I felt a deep sense of longing to experience the ritual and ceremony of marriage. Thinking back to the former soul's twenty-two-year marriage, I smiled as I knew that I was not opposed to marriage itself, just opposed to the person that she had chosen to wed.

As I looked upon this opening to my Decree to God, I was wondering what to write next when the pen snapped to attention in my hand and immediately began to automatically write the next line on its own:

"I live in a comfortable home near the ocean."

Never having performed automatic writing before, and not knowing where this had come from, I broke out in laughter. I was renting a one-bedroom apartment across from the ocean, but I certainly didn't have the means to afford to buy my own home. After I registered the thought of living in an oceanfront home, the pen came alive again

186

and both of us wrote the wonderful characteristics and attributes that my Twin-Flame possessed.

We wrote that he was kind, gentle, considerate, loyal, trusting, responsible and reliable, and he treated me like a princess. He had a great sense of humour and made me laugh. We were supportive of one another, and loved to work and travel the world together. We were the best of friends as well as cherished lovers and nothing took priority over our relationship. We respected and allowed each other to be who we were without seeking to change each other in any way. I also wrote that he spoke Italian.

At the end of the letter, the pen wrote:

"I have a wonderful, successful healing practice and my clients love me and refer me to others."

At this stage, I had never considered studying any alternative or holistic therapies. Having finished writing, I sat in silence as I tried to absorb what had just happened. Seeing this decree as a very sacred, important declaration that I had made to God, I decided to give it the honour it deserved. I slept with it under my pillow and every morning and evening I lovingly and emotionally read it aloud. Yet, I didn't just read the words 'parrot fashion.' I felt what it would be like to laugh together, to snuggle on the couch watching movies, and to hold hands as we walked in front of our oceanfront home together.

In addition to honouring my dreams of being with my Twin-Flame, I instinctively knew of the great importance of honouring and nurturing myself physically, mentally, emotionally and spiritually. This included doing things that made me happy and gave me great joy.

Feeling as if I had come home to my true self, I felt a great urge inside to take a trip back to the States and to reconnect with my biological family. From the moment I arrived, my parents and brothers could see that I was a very different Candy compared to the one they were used to. They saw for the first time someone who was self-assured, confident and independent. Presenting myself as empowered did not gel at all with the Candy that they remembered. With their daughter being highly co-dependent her entire life, now that I was newly separated from R, my parents were naturally very concerned as to what my plans were and what I was going to do now that I was on my own. After all, the only Candy they had ever known had allowed others to take care of her.

During my three weeks in the States, my parents suggested that while I was on holiday, it would be nice if I could spend a few days with my brother in New Jersey. Instantly, my intuitive nature clearly picked up that they were panicking as to what was to be done with me now that I was no longer attached to a man. Driving up to New Jersey with my brother, he casually dropped into the conversation that now that I was single, he knew lots of rich, divorced men through his medical practice. I told him that when I meet someone, it was not going to happen in that way. He said, "What have you got to lose? Why don't you spend a day with one of these eligible bachelors and just see how it turns out?"

High on my brother's list of possible suitors was a divorced, Jewish dentist by the name of T. Against all of my instincts and better judgment, I agreed to the date. T phoned that evening and arranged to pick me up for breakfast and spend the next day together. The following morning brought a beautiful, early spring day. The sun was shining brightly and there was a cool, crisp quality in the air. As he had planned, T rang the doorbell at precisely 9 a.m. Opening the door, I was presented with a gentleman with a full head of white hair in his late fifties, proudly grinning and showing off a gleaming set of dentures. Introducing himself, he suggested we go to his favorite place for breakfast.

Immediately upon starting his car, T launched into telling me about his successful dentistry practice and how much money he was making. I listened amiably and when I tried to speak, he spoke on top of me. I thought that perhaps he was a little hard of hearing, and so I gently raised the volume of my voice, but to no avail. He didn't seem to be interested in listening to anything I had to say. Driving onto the highway, we passed several exits. I asked him if the restaurant was far away and he informed me that we were almost there. Up in the distance, I saw a huge sign for a truck stop. Pulling his car into the parking lot, he proudly exclaimed, "We're here!"

Getting out of the car, I thought for sure this was a practical joke that my brother had set up. Walking into the truck stop, a waitress led us to a scratched Formica table. As we sat down, T leaned over to me and whispered, "Order one of the specials; they are cheaper." This place obviously must have had shares in pork bellies because everything came with extra bacon. When the waitress appeared, T said he would have the $3.99 special with bottomless coffee. At the mention of the word 'bottomless,' he paused and winked at me as if to say, *"This is a good deal, you should get the same."*

Searching high and low through the menu, I couldn't find any of the specials that were to my liking as I was a vegetarian, so I ordered toast, two fried eggs and a cup of tea.

Tapping me on the sleeve, as if one would castigate a child who had made a mistake, he slowly explained, "You know, if you ordered a # 4 special, it would be cheaper and you could get hash browns, sausage, and bacon with it." Looking at him calmly, I said, "No thank you," and re-stated my order to the waitress.

Turning his attention to his bottomless cup of coffee, T started telling me what was wrong with the American political situation and how the Jews always get it in the end. At the mention of the word 'Jew,' his face became twisted and he appeared as if he was in pain.

As before, I tried to enter into the conversation, but much like a beginning driver trying to merge with rush hour traffic, my attempts were all but ignored. Speaking with his mouth full, a piece of bacon escaped from his lips and poked from his mouth like a tongue. "So what do you want to do the rest of the day?" Trying to avert my eyes from the tongue-like bacon, I explained that, as I was in New York for such a short time, I would love to catch the train into the city and see a Broadway matinee. I suggested that perhaps afterwards, we could have an early dinner and then catch the train back.

He seemed distant and disinterested as I spoke. Half-heartedly he agreed, although he was quick to point out that on the way to the station, he would have to swing by his dental practice. Leaving the truck stop around 10 a.m., we drove twenty minutes and arrived at his office. Getting out of the car, he said he was so smart to have bought into this building years before because it was now a sought-after site for businesses and professionals.

Upon entering, he told me that his secretary had been given the day off, so he had to come in and check his messages. T walked into his office at the back and began replaying his voice mail messages. Just then, the door opened and a gentleman walked in holding his cheek. Assuming that I was T's receptionist, he said that he had an appointment with the dentist. Realizing the gentleman's mistake, I replied that I was not the receptionist but that I would inform him. Going into T's office, I said, "There must be some mistake. There is someone here who insists that he has an appointment with you now. Is that right?" Reacting as if his real motives for the office visit had been found out, he said that he really had to see this patient and it wouldn't take too long.

Sitting out in the waiting room, I started reading the magazines. An hour and a half later, T poked his head around the corner, saying that it wouldn't be much longer. Finally, around 12:30 p.m., the patient emerged, rather sore and sorry, wrote out a check and left the office. Taking off his white coat, T said. "I'm really sorry about that, it couldn't be helped," although the tone of his voice sounded anything but sorry. With an upbeat tone, he said, "Oh well, looks like we won't be able to see that show after all; we just won't be able to make it in time. Why don't I show you around the Princeton University campus instead?"

Although I was quite disappointed that I wouldn't be seeing a show, I was ecstatic just to be out of his office. Stepping outside, I breathed deeply and welcomed the fresh air. Driving around the campus was beautiful and we stopped to take a stroll around the cute little cafés and shops. Once more, he dominated the conversation about his divorce and how his terrible ex-wife had ruined his life. Again, I tried to respond with empathy and compassion, but he seemed to be so consumed by the sound of his own voice that he took no notice of what I was saying.

Passing by a Borders bookstore, he said that he needed to go in and look up a title. As he walked toward the history section, I said that I would look up some books as well. Escaping to a different area of the store, I quickly hurried to the New Age section and, while browsing interesting metaphysical titles, I befriended a like-minded store assistant. We were engaged in a great discussion of spirituality, when I was startled by T's indignant tone behind me. "I had no idea that you were into *that* sort of stuff!" A heavy emphasis of disapproval had been put on the word 'that'.

It was just on the tip of my tongue to say, *"If you had shown me some consideration by letting me speak and had tried to find out something about me, I guess it wouldn't have come as such a surprise to find out what my preferences and interests were."* But I didn't.

Walking outside, I discovered the sun had disappeared. A cold wind had picked up and was swirling fallen, dead leaves across the ground. I noted that the chill in the air was mirroring my cold feelings towards this bitter, self-centered, self-absorbed man. Feeling a chill in my bones I said, "Why don't we go for a hot drink?" Passing by many cute cafés, I suggested that we go in and warm up but T said to wait because there were others coming up. Finally, he bought me a tea at a convenience store and we sat outside in the cold. Conversation was very strained and we nursed our hot drinks in almost total silence. With a sigh, he glanced at his watch, noted that it was 4 o'clock and announced that it was much too early for dinner.

Wanting to get out of the bitter chill, I suggested that we go to the movies. Completely ignoring me again, he said that we should drive to his place and listen to some music. I agreed to this plan, thinking perhaps he would be more comfortable in his own surroundings.

Driving into a gated community and passing rows and rows of identical townhouses, he grumbled that he used to own a large, beautiful home, but 'the wife' took everything in the divorce. As he mentioned the words, 'the wife,' he gagged as if he was going to throw up. As I got out of the car and approached the front door, T stopped me and said, "When I open the door, you stay outside while I go in. They like to be alerted when there is a stranger coming."

Not having the slightest idea as to what or whom he was talking about, I remained outside. As he entered the house he called, "Simba! Misty! We have a guest." Turning around, he signaled for me to come closer and pointed upwards towards the second floor landing where two enormous cats were staring down at us. As I walked in, the pungent smell of cat urine hit me in the face. T nudged me forward and said, "Go in, don't be shy, and make yourself comfortable."

Stifling my desire to be sick, I walked into a large lounge room that contained only three things: a couch, a recliner rocker and a stereo system. Both pieces of furniture had claw marks where they had been scratched and torn by the cats. Old, worn blankets infused with cat fur were draped across the surface of the chair and the sofa. Sitting as close to the edge of the sofa as possible without falling off, I tried to avoid contact with the cat fur. As soon as T slumped into the recliner, both cats descended upon him. He then proceeded to cuddle and talk to them, totaling ignoring me. As he asked them if they had had a nice day and inquiring as to what things they did, I felt myself becoming envious of the cats, as this was more than he asked me in the whole time we had spent together.

After having a conversation with the cats, he got up and walked into the kitchen. The open plan design of the room afforded me a view directly into the kitchen area and I watched as the cats jumped up onto the counter. T took a large jar of pretzels out of the cupboard, grabbed a handful, gave some to the cats and stuffed the rest in his mouth. He then took another handful and walked over to the stereo. The cats came tearing into the room and darted around his legs. Speaking with his mouth full of pretzels he asked me, "What kind of music do you like?"

I was taken aback that he actually inquired about something that I liked. Being agreeable, I said, "I like all different kinds of music, but I like classical music the best because I learned to play many of the pieces on the piano."

Bits of pretzel flew from his mouth as he abruptly and angrily replied, "As far as I'm concerned, there is only one kind of music worth listening to and that's the music of the seventies. That was the happiest time of my life, before I married my miserable ex, and I don't listen to anything else."

Deciding between Leo Sayer, Gloria Gaynor and the Bee Gees, he proceeded to put on some Donna Summer disco music and flopped down on the recliner. Both cats immediately pounced on him and he resumed his conversation with them. I kept looking at my watch and praying for time to pass quickly. For one hour, T did not offer me a drink – no coffee, no tea, nor anything to eat. At about 5:30 p.m., he said that we should leave for dinner. Absolutely thrilled, I grabbed my coat and hurried out the door.

He said that we would go to his favorite Chinese restaurant, which was not far from his house. We turned into a strip shopping mall and parked in front of gaily-lit Chinese lanterns decorating what appeared to be a Chinese take-away. We were shown to a table and sat down. Looking over the menu, T said that the dishes were very large, so we should order only one dish and a large white rice to share between the two of us. Knowing that this peculiar day was almost at an end, I quickly agreed; I was far too famished to say anything.

Politely, I asked him what dishes he liked to eat. Looking around the restaurant and anywhere else but in my direction, he replied, "I make a point of only eating white foods: bean sprouts, rice, chicken, water chestnuts and cauliflower."

Interested in his choice of foods, I asked him if these were due to dietary concerns. In an irritated manner he said, "No, I just find it easier to deal with when ordering." There was only one dish on the menu that suited his rather individual preferences. The day had been such an odd series of events that I agreed to his choice of meal.

Seeing the waiter approaching us, T leaned over to me and

quickly said, "When the waiter takes our order, ask me about my advertising budget for my business."

Before I had time to register such a strange request, the waiter appeared, so I said, "So, how is the advertising campaign coming along for your dentistry practice this year?"

He then placed our order and, as the waiter left, he triumphantly announced, "That's great, now I can write this dinner off on my taxes and put it down as a business expense."

Horrified, I sat there in disbelief. The rest of dinner, as well as the ride home, was spent in silence. I was so happy to see the end of this bizarre date.

The next day, my brother said that T had called him and told him that I was not what he was looking for. He said that I was a nice enough girl, but that I didn't have anything to say for myself! I recounted to my parents the day that I had spent with my brother's choice of a so-called 'eligible' bachelor.

With the time approaching for my scheduled return flight to Australia, my parents asked me to remain in the States as I seemingly had nothing to go back to. I then replied, "I don't have anything to go back to now, but something in my heart is telling me not to remain in the States and to return to Australia."

As I boarded the Qantas flight, I felt like I was going home. Even with no relationship and no job to return to, I had an overwhelming feeling that I was returning to fulfill my destiny.

18

Your Wish Is Fulfilled

After returning to Australia, I synchronistically bumped into Diane, a former customer from my café, who was a nurse. Upon seeing me, she looked into my eyes and said, "You have undergone a great transformation since I saw you last year. It is like you are a new person."

When I asked her how she was, I was surprised to hear that she had been busy attuning many students to Reiki, as I did not know that she was a Reiki Teacher. Upon her utterance of the word Reiki, I felt a shiver of confirmation go through my body, as I remembered Mel's words to me: "Reiki will become very important to you."

When I asked her about teaching Reiki, Diane told me that she was a fifth generation clairvoyant, and that she had established her Reiki Academy many years ago. Sensing a very different energy within me now compared to what I was previously like when I owned the café, Diane said, "My guides and angels are telling me that it is very important for you to learn Reiki." She hesitated as she tuned into the messages that she was receiving. "And the angels are telling me that I cannot charge you."

I will be forever grateful to my Reiki Master/Teacher Diane McCormick, and her wonderful husband Michael for providing me a safe harbour during those early months after my Walk-In experience.

Diane and I were two kindred spirits who spent long days studying, laughing, and discussing all things metaphysical. I was often asked to stay for dinner and, in this way, I was fed not only spiritually but physically as well. Not being grounded at all, I would often forget to eat for several days at a time and my weight dropped even further. Just because one finds out that one has had a Walk-In experience, it does not make it any easier to adjust to doing human things again, like eating.

It was during this time of study with Diane, that I asked Michael if he knew of a financial advisor that I could speak with concerning the investment of my divorce settlement. Referring me to a friend of his who worked close to where I lived, I made an appointment the following week. As the date drew closer, I received a phone call from this advisor asking me if I minded meeting him at his other office that was close to an hour away. The logical thing to do would have been to reschedule, but my intuitive urging told me to keep the initial appointment.

I drove the hour to the financial advisor's office and was surprised to find myself in an area that I had not been before. As we discussed the various options as to where I could invest my money, I kept getting distracted by the many flags and signs that were prominently displayed outside of a new shopping complex across the street. At the end of our meeting, I gathered up the notes that I had made and told him that I would be in touch. Leaving his office, I had a strong urge to go browsing through the new shopping mall.

As I entered the mall, I looked at the directory and saw that most of the stores were on the higher levels but I felt a pressing urge to go down to the basement. As the elevator door opened, I saw that this level contained services like the post office, Medicare, a bank and a pharmacy. It was then that I saw a small sign pointing around a corner that read, 'Your Divine Destiny'. Upon reading the sign, I received shivers up and down my spine, and I followed the arrow. At the end of the corridor, I saw Tibetan flags surrounding the entrance to a New Age shop.

When I entered the store, the girl behind the counter cheerfully said, "Hi, Mirabelle will be ready in just a minute."

When I enquired as to who Mirabelle was, she said that she was the psychic reader for the day. Upon hearing this, another series of shivers shot through my body and suddenly, a large woman walked into the room and gestured for me to come over to her. Feeling as if some energetic force was drawing me over to her table, I sat down.

She told me to pick eleven cards from her Tarot deck. As I was choosing the cards, she said, "You have undergone a great shift within." Staring intently at me, her light green eyes seemed to be on fire, as her gaze felt like she was looking directly into my soul.

She then continued without even glancing at her cards, "You have come from another realm, the Angelic Realm and your mission is very great." Taking the cards that I had drawn, she looked at them and smiled. "My dear, sweet child, your wish is fulfilled. Did you know that you are supposed to be meeting your Twin-Flame?" I smiled and said that I knew that he was coming.

All of a sudden, a dark cloud seemed to appear on Mirabelle's face, and it completely changed her expression. With great seriousness, she said, "In your present condition, he will never be able to see you and your meeting will never take place. You do not have one ounce of body fat on your anorexic frame, as you choose to not eat and you live primarily in the etheric world. You are of the Earth now and you must eat, my dear child. Go home, fatten up, gain weight, then, and only then, will he be able to see your physical form." Looking down at my cards again, she cautioned, "Heed their warning!"

When I enquired as to whether there were any other messages they wished to give me, Mirabelle replied, "You two have a very sacred mission of God indeed. Once you meet your Twin-Flame, all else will fall into place."

As I took out my wallet and asked her how much I owed her for the reading, she replied with smiling eyes, "There will be no charge." From that moment on, I could not stop stuffing food into my mouth and slowly my skeletal body started to fill out.

197

In June 2003, the prophecy that the pen had automatically written into my sacred decree about owning my own healing practice became a reality as I completed all levels of Reiki, including the Mastership and the Teaching Degree. The day after I received my Reiki degrees, I applied for my business license and decided to establish my Reiki healing practice in my lovely little one-bedroom apartment. Buying a hand painted screen, I used it to partition off part of the lounge room and began to see clients. I synchronistically began to bump into the many people that I had as customers from the café and told them about my new business. In support of this Divine purpose, the Universe began to magically present me with the people and the situations that I needed to build up my practice. Within a short space of time my clientele increased, as people would enthusiastically refer me to their friends and family.

Throwing all my passion into my business, the next month seemed to fly by. With July fast approaching, I took note that the lease for my apartment was coming up for renewal. Yet, something inside of me hesitated this time when I thought about renewing my lease for another three months.

Having seen clients in my lounge room for the past month, I thought that, if I was really going to respect my chosen path and be seen as a professional, then I should start looking for a two-bedroom apartment. In this way, I could make one bedroom into a healing room. Suddenly I received a shower of tingles as an all-over confirmation that it was time to look for a new place to live.

As I was pondering how I was going to afford a two-bedroom apartment, I heard the words, *'Do not worry, all will be well.'* The next day, I was invited over to Robyn's for lunch and I told her that I was feeling like it was time to move. With great excitement, she said that there were vacancies in her building, but she added that, with it being Sunday, the management office was closed. We giggled as we imagined what it would be like knocking on each other's doors in our pajamas and hanging out together.

Excitedly leaving her house, I thought I would drive around and explore the area where I hoped my new apartment would be. As soon as this thought came into my head, I heard the words, *'TURN LEFT'*. I turned down a short road that wound its way along a canal and at the end was an apartment building. On the grass, there was a sign that read 'Apartment for Rent' with a phone number. I quickly called on my mobile and enquired about the rent. It was a double apartment and the rental price was $500 a week. At that stage it was way above my budget as I was currently paying $320.

As I drove home, the late afternoon Gold Coast sun cast long shadows on the road. For some reason, Michael, the real estate agent, popped into my head. Although late in the day, I knew he would still be working. Sure enough, as I drove into the agency's parking lot, his car was the only one there. As I opened the door, Michael looked up while speaking on the phone and his face beamed as I walked in. He smiled broadly and indicated that he would be just a minute. While waiting for him, I picked up the latest rental list and there, on the top, was this ad:

Large, spacious two-bedroom unit with balcony overlooking view of the canal—$270.

As Michael got off the phone, he came over and rather amorously planted a kiss on my cheek. Ignoring the kiss, I asked him about the apartment. He said it had just been listed a few hours before and nobody had viewed it as yet. I told him it sounded too good to be true as I had been paying $320 for a one-bedroom unit. He gave me a rental application to fill out and suggested I drive first thing in the morning to their other rental office and ask for the keys to look at the apartment. I asked Michael where the apartment was and he said on Canal Street in Runaway Bay. I thanked him and left.

Again, my intuition told me, *'Why wait until tomorrow morning? Drive to the address now and see where the apartment is located.'* Looking up the street address, I began to drive to Runaway Bay and noticed that I was backtracking to Robyn's house. Following the directions, I turned right into Canal Street and got the shock of my life. It was the same street my intuition had led me to earlier and it was in the same complex where I noticed the sign for the $500 apartment. Having just been listed several hours previously, it was too new a listing to have been given a rental sign. But with this kind of confirmation, I truly did not need any signs other than the ones I was receiving from God.

The apartment was stunning, and by the end of the following day, it was mine. It was also unfurnished. This would be my next huge step towards expressing my independence. Inviting my lovely friend Robyn, we went on a shopping spree. For the first time in my life, I made independent decisions on furniture, matching towels, plates, and cutlery – absolutely everything. My purchases were beautiful and reflected the beauty I truly felt as if I had been given a new lease on life. Little did I know how enormously my life was about to change even more.

19

Stevie Nicks Meets Elvis

After moving in and coordinating the new furnishings in my beautiful apartment, I felt an urge to entertain. Sitting down on the purple, brushed suede couch, I noticed how bare it was and thought it could use some colourful throw pillows. I was about to make a note to buy some cushions, when I heard an emphatic voice speaking to me loud and clear: *'No! Be creative'*. With my newfound psychic awareness, it had become commonplace for me to discern the voice of God speaking to me. As I considered His idea of being creative rather than just buying pillows, I immediately thought that it would be much quicker and more time-efficient to just go out and buy some.

Immediately, the tone of the voice became firmer and more adamant. *'NO! BE CREATIVE!'* Having been gently but firmly persuaded to change my mind, I remembered that I loved craftwork. Yet with all the changes that had happened in my life, I had all but forgotten my artistic pursuits. Envisioning the finished cushions on the couch, I remembered that I had always wanted to learn the art of silk ribbon floral designs and thought that silk roses would look lovely on the pillows.

The next day, while I was having coffee with my dear friend Val, she told me about a new sewing shop that had recently opened and it was only ten minutes away from my new apartment. In addition to selling sewing and embroidery items at the front of the shop, the owner gave sewing lessons at the back. Val and I decided to learn how to make silk flowers and after several weeks, I had produced two beautiful patterns of roses. However, I am not a seamstress and I needed a dressmaker to make the patterns into pillows. Excitedly, Val suggested a great dressmaker nearby named Donna-May, who lived only one block away from me.

Entering Donna-May's home, I told her that she had been highly recommended. Asking her how long she would need to make the designs into pillows, she said it was an easy job and it would only take three days. Asking for my details, I pulled out one of my business cards and handed it to her. In an excited voice, she said that she had just been speaking to a friend about finding a Reiki Practitioner and that she would get her to give me a call. I returned three days later, and she was very apologetic, as she hadn't had time to sew my pillows. But she did say that she had a few more friends who wanted Reiki sessions with me. After four weeks, and many new clients, she still had not completed the pillows. This time, however, she said, "I'm so sorry I haven't sewn your pillows yet. You are such a patient, lovely person. Would you like to come to my party on Saturday night?" Without hesitating, I said, "Sure!"

She then added, "But there is a catch – it is a 'Come as Your Favourite Rock Star' party!" I used the left over materials from my pillows and created a headpiece of flowing ribbons and silk flowers. I then bought a diaphanous, purple goddess top and I went as Stevie Nicks from Fleetwood Mac.

On my way to the party I stopped off at a bottle shop, as the invitation asked for guests to bring their own drinks. Standing in a long line of men cradling their cases of beer and bottles of spirits, I waited patiently with my laurel wreath of flowers, leaves and ribbons cascading down my long, curly hair. One of the men looked at me and said, "Hey, we have a princess here." While the other men laughed, he added, "Wherever you are going, you're gonna have a magical night."

A thunderbolt of shivers shot through my body and the

aftershocks continued as I drove to the party. And that is how I happened to be nursing a drink at the stragglers table at Donna-May's party on Saturday, September 20, 2003.

As I looked at the sea of unfamiliar faces and inventive costumes, I wondered what in the hell I was doing there, as I knew no one else. The party had started at 6 p.m. and within half an hour, I had decided to stay for only thirty minutes more before I would make my excuses and leave. But, on the stroke of 7 p.m., a tall, lanky Elvis appeared in the doorway that opened to the back verandah where the party was held. This Elvis was complete with an all-in-one white jumpsuit, large, gold belt buckle, red cape, pompadour hairdo and aviator glasses. With the indoor lighting behind him shining out towards the darkened low-lit verandah, it gave the appearance of a shining spotlight illuminating and heralding his entrance.

Pete would later say that the only people he knew were at the other end of the verandah, but as he tried to move closer to them, he felt as if his feet were stuck in cement. A guy on our table shouted, "Hey, Elvis is in the house. Grab a chair and sit down here," and so Pete joined us.

In between embarrassing but fun karaoke attempts and dinner, we gravitated towards one another and spent the next five hours talking. There was an ease of conversation and we were obviously quite taken with each other. At one stage, Pete looked down and said, "This is not a 'come on' line but you have beautiful hands." (I hadn't yet told him about my work as a Healing Practitioner.)

Looking at my watch, I saw that it was quickly approaching midnight. Not wanting our time together to end, I asked him what he was doing the next day. He said that he planned to go to church in the morning and visit a friend in the afternoon but he didn't feel like doing either of those as he would much rather see me. We both agreed to meet the next morning.

Asking if he could walk me to my car, we shared our first kiss in the moonlight. I turned the key to drive away, but, if truth be known, I could have flown home myself as I felt so lighthearted, excited and happy.

I woke early the next morning to get ready for Pete's arrival at 9:30 a.m. Standing by the second floor window in the common area of my apartment building, I had a bird's-eye view down the road to the end of the cul-de-sac. As I gazed out in anticipation, it occurred to me that I didn't know what type of car he drove. But even more incredibly, I had no idea what he really looked like, as I had only seen him in costume!! With each car that came down the road, my heart skipped a beat. There were five cars, each turning around at the end of the cul-de-sac, before a silver Commodore stopped in front of the building. Getting out of the car stepped a dark, handsome, lanky guy; but so very handsome. The rest of the day floated by as if time stood still. It was not only the flow of conversation that was noticeable, but there was a natural ease of familiarity and comfort that is usually found in long-standing, established friendships.

We told each other about ourselves. Pete was thirty-seven years old, had never been married and had no children. I was completely honest and told that him that I was forty-seven, had been married once before and had two grown children. Yet, I also disclosed to him openly about my angelic Walk-In experience. We spent a heavenly day and Pete ended up staying the night.

The next morning, sitting on my sun-drenched balcony while sipping coffee, Pete said, "I really need to say something. Yesterday was such a wonderful day, and you are such a beautiful person; but here is what I am looking for. I am looking for a girl in her mid-twenties and we can date for a couple of years before getting engaged, then, after a couple of years, get married and after a year or two we can have two or three kids."

All the time he was speaking, I was staring at him, knowing full well that he was the Twin-Flame that I had thanked God for. Without interrupting him, I let him finish his speech. He said that he had some appointments at the southern end of the coast but asked if it would be okay if he dropped in late afternoon on his way back through to the Sunshine Coast. I said sure, and we kissed goodbye. Standing by the large window in the hall, I watched him get into his car and drive off.

I'm not sure how I spent the rest of that day, but the minutes ticked by very slowly until he reappeared on my doorstep late that afternoon. Although he had only intended to stay for coffee, that became dinner and he ended up staying another night. The following morning, we found ourselves back on my balcony once again sipping coffee. Pete said, "This is ridiculous! I have work to do back home, but I don't want to go."

Looking at him, I said, "I don't want you to go."

Immediately he replied, "Do you want to come with me?"

Now, I am usually the kind of person who has to organize in advance for a trip away; coordinating outfits, shoes and bags and packing the right toiletries can take weeks to organize. Without hesitation I said, "Yes!" I jumped out of my seat, ran to the bedroom and began throwing whatever I could get my hands on into a suitcase. Putting another smaller bag at the end of the vanity in the bathroom, I literally swept my hand across the shelf and filled the bag with cosmetics and toiletries. Hurriedly, I closed the suitcase with my clothes sticking out of the side, along with the cord from my blow dryer. Within fifteen minutes, I was sitting in his car, buckling my seatbelt and heading two-and-a-half hours north to the Sunshine Coast. I had only the briefest flash of a thought that he could possibly be an axe murderer and that my head would be found in a freezer somewhere! Tuning in to The Posse of Angels, I received a resounding, "NO!"

On our drive, we listened to music, laughed and chatted with ease. I did make a mental note that there seemed to be an air of expectation, as if I was returning to some place that I had known before. The song *My Happiness* by the Aussie band Powderfinger was playing on a CD and I was overwhelmed by its prophetic lyrics:

... It seems an age since I've seen you ... So you come in and put your bags down ... I know there's something in the air ... My happiness is slowly creeping back,

Now you're at home ...

As we drove into his community of lovely homes, Pete explained to me that the builder of his house had incorporated Feng Shui principles in its design. I absolutely loved the windowed atrium with white pebbles, bamboo plants and a fountain built into the centre of the home. With an open and airy feel, the house had such beautiful, light energies. After carrying my bag in, Pete was excited to take me on a walk. Exiting his backyard gate, we found ourselves on a path in a grassy reserve, which meandered down to a boardwalk and took us through a paper bark forest. I did not tell Pete, but I could clearly see the faeries that were living there. Within two minutes, we walked out of the forest and were standing on a pristine stretch of beautiful, white sandy beach along the ocean.

I can't recall exactly what we did Tuesday and Wednesday but I do remember what happened on Thursday, a mere five days after we met. Sitting in bed together, Pete turned to me and felt compelled to ask, "Will you marry me?" The enormity and the importance of that question took him by surprise.

I immediately answered, "Yes." We embraced and, after a moment, I said, "But it's not a proper proposal unless you're on your knee." This formality was important to me. Having never received a formal proposal from my ex, I had missed out, as I had asked him to marry me. It was then that Pete hopped out of bed, came around to my side, knelt down and asked me again.

"Yes – of course, yes."

Pete would later say that it had occurred to him to propose on the third day after we met, but that he thought he should wait. As it turned out, he could wait only two days more!

People ask me how I could have said yes after knowing Pete for only five days. In fact, I knew intuitively that we had danced this wonderful dance many times before and that he was the Twin-Flame that I had asked for in my sacred decree that I had written to God.

Having just signed a long-term lease for my new apartment, I needed Divine intervention to find someone to take over my lease. Calling the rental agency, I told them that I had become engaged and I was now looking to re-let my new apartment. The rental agent said, in an astonished voice, "We just had someone in the office looking for a two-bedroom unit on the canal. Would it be alright if they could come over and have a look at the unit this afternoon?"

Ten days later, after finding someone to take over my lease, I moved my furniture into Pete's home. As if by magic, everything that I had bought was a perfect fit – and I mean perfect! My entertainment stand that I had purchased six weeks earlier fit into an alcove in the wall of Pete's lounge room with a mere half-inch to spare on either side. It was as if I had unconsciously picked out furniture for my *future* home!

It was eight weeks later, two months after we met, that we were married on the beach in Noosa Heads, Queensland, Australia. It was just myself, Pete, the pastor and two witnesses. (Actually, with only weeks before the wedding, the pastor asked us who our witnesses were going to be and we both said, "What witnesses? Do we really need them?" as we did not know it but, by law there must be at least two. So we quickly asked a best mate of Pete's and the jeweler who had made our wedding rings. Our fairy tale life together had only just begun.

Looking back on how Pete and I had met, I always thought that it was rather strange that Donna-May had invited me to her party; as it had turned out to be her engagement party. One usually only invites cherished friends and family to their engagement, yet we had only met three times before.

And what ever happened to those pillows, you may ask? Well, it was eight months later that Pete and I decided to take a trip back to the Gold Coast to visit friends. I told him that those pillows were sentimental to me and that I wanted to stop in at Donna-May's to pick them up. Walking in to her home, we discovered that *the pillows still were not finished!* I realized that the reason that they were never completed was because my intuition, which had told me to BE CREATIVE, had nothing to do with the pillows. Donna-May and

Pete are related; she is his sister-in-law's sister. As family, he was invited to her engagement party and the creating of those pillows was always only about meeting my beloved Pete.

The following week, after I had picked up the unfinished flower designs, I took them to a local seamstress in my new area on the Sunshine Coast and asked her how long it would take to make them into pillows. When she said, "Three days," I couldn't stop laughing. But, when I went back after three days, this time, they were finished.

To this day, those pillows are proudly displayed in my home and stand testament to what can happen when one faithfully follows the voice of God.

20

Our Twin-Flame Mission Revealed

After our wedding, Pete and I celebrated our Earth incarnation reunion by going on a heavenly trip to the Whitsunday Islands along the Great Barrier Reef in Queensland, Australia. We nestled for a week in a bungalow on the ocean's edge at the honeymoon resort Peppers Palm Bay on Long Island. No phones, no computers and no TV saw us spending our days kayaking, fishing and swimming in the clear, turquoise waters. One day we took a seaplane to the magnificent, pure white sands of Whitehaven Beach where we were treated to a champagne lunch and then flew out to the reef for an unbelievable snorkeling experience.

Upon arriving back home on the Sunshine Coast, we began our next dance as husband and wife. I say 'next dance' as I, Angel Ariel and Pete, Kiel, have been together in many lifetimes. One of the most favourite lives that we have shared was thirty-two thousand years ago, when Pete and I were Aborigines in the northern region of Western Australia, known as the Kimberley. We were husband and wife and looked after a sacred well with our sixteen children. Living off the land, we were happy and fulfilled as we were provided with everything that we ever needed.

Turning my attention to my beautiful new home, I remembered what the pen had foretold when it wrote in my Decree to God, '*I live in a comfortable home near the ocean'.* I began to cry, as I was overwhelmed with gratitude for the blessings that I had been given in my life. Walking into my office filled with angel statues and crystals, I sat down at my altar, lit candles and bowed my head. I thanked God for my blessed new heavenly life and I said aloud, "Show me how I can serve. I will, to will Thy will."

Immediately the room temperature began to drop and, although it was a hot summer's day, it became so cold that I could see my breath. The room then began to fill up with angels; tall shards of light became visible as they stepped forward from the Etheric Realm and presented themselves to me. Each angel bent down and, as a gesture of respect and recognition for a fellow angel, they bowed their head and gently touched their forehead to mine. The deep love and heartfelt connection that they conveyed radiated God's pure light and waves of angels filled the room.

Next, the Archangels stepped forward into physical form. Archangel Michael brought in the strength of his indigo blue. Archangel Gabriel painted the room a soft, sky blue. Both Archangel Uriel and Archangel Jophiel washed the room in sunny, bright yellow. Archangel Raphael transformed the room to a deep, healing green. Then, Archangel Haniel sprinkled bursts of silver that filled the room and Archangel Chamuel bathed everything in the palest pink and the scent of rose petals filled the air.

Lastly, there was a burst of blue light as Mother Mary stepped forward on my left and Mary Magdalene stepped forward on my right. The room then began to illuminate with a golden glow and Jesus stepped forward between the two women.

Speaking in one voice, they said, "We are your collective of five-hundred-and-thirty-seven and we will be with you for the duration of your physical incarnation in service to the Divine. Our collective group, The Posse of Angels, will never be any less nor any more than five-hundred-and-thirty-seven, as this is a very significant number energetically to assist you on your mission."

It was later on that I found out the significance of that number

537. With the number five signifying change and challenges, I would help others challenge and change their perceptions of angels and what is possible beyond their limited physical senses.

As the number three represents creation, alchemical magic and the physical, tangible manifestation of aligning and working with the Divine, I would be helping others to connect to their ancient spiritual wisdom and their own powers of magic within.

And lastly, the number seven represents a spiritual journey in service to God and signifies Divine perfection, completion and unity. As Angel Ariel in service to the Divine, I will be the physical representation of God's pure essence, reflecting onto others their own Divine nature.

After The Posse of Angels revealed themselves, a faint chorus of beautiful voices filled the room as the vision began to fade. Overcome with joy, I sat quietly. Thinking back over my journey from Spirit into physical form, I began to feel enormous pressure as to how I was going to be of best service to God. Feeling as if I was wrapped in a warm blanket of assurance, The Posse of Angels said, "Do not worry, dear one. Your mission and all that is asked of you will happen if you remember to do one thing. Every time God asks you to step forward, simply follow His word and say yes. The miracles that you two have Divinely contracted to bring forth, will appear. All you need to do is to listen, trust, be faithful children of God, and allow yourselves to be led."

As this knowledge settled on my heart, I felt the restriction in my chest release and I smiled knowing that the next phase of my amazing journey as Walk-In Angel Ariel on the Earth plane was just beginning.

THE END ...

... and the beginning.

Epilogue

As I completed *I Am an Angelic Walk-In*, I began to feel a very strong, familiar presence around me. The former soul, Claire Candy, who was in the body prior to the Walk-In experience on January 11, 2003, had eagerly anticipated the completion of this sequel; as so much of what I wrote was an accounting of her life. In many ways, I felt like a dedicated biographer who wishes to remain true to someone who has crossed over. Yet, instead of interviewing other people, I had the great advantage of conversing freely with my subject across the veil.

I graciously thank the former soul, Claire Candy, who kept me on track, added personal details and clarified elements of her life when needed. The reason her presence felt stronger was because she had a favour to ask of me – she wished to write the epilogue to 'our' story. When I asked her if I had been thorough and correct in the retelling of her life, she smiled and said that I had been very accurate. Her wish to write an epilogue was not to correct or add anything to her story, but to impart what she learned as a result of the life that she had led. For as the first novel, *One True Home – Behind the Veil of Forgetfulness* clearly shows us, it is not the particulars of each life that matters most, but what we learn from each incarnation and how much we allow ourselves to grow as a result of our experiences.

Dear Readers,

Hi, my name is Claire Candy and I chose to be in human incarnation, born on October 7, 1955, until I chose to exit my contract early, or walk out, on January 11, 2003. Firstly, I must give praise to my teacher, Angel Ariel who now embodies Claire Candy Hough, for being a faithful steward in writing a truthful recounting of my life in physical form. On one hand, I was not surprised as she had inherited my memory imprint, but she truly listened to me with great sensitivity and was able to compassionately convey what I felt through my experiences as a wife, mother and daughter.

When I first found out that this book was going to be written, I immediately felt vindicated, as others would finally understand the unexplained, enormous changes that I went through and why I chose to exit my life early. After years and years of systematic bullying and silent mental and emotional abuse, I guess I did not have enough reserve strength left in the tank to wait until the tide changed. (From the heightened vantage point that I now occupy across the veil, one can clearly see that the tide always changes.) Yet, the more I attended Spiritual School and began to see the life I lived from a very different perspective, I realized that I did not need to feel vindicated by anybody. Yet this clarity of mine has only just recently happened.

You see, it has not been long since I was strong enough to regain my light and go through the transition levels of Heaven that everyone goes through from physical flesh to returning to our one true home in Spirit. I had been so traumatized and devoid of light while in human form that when I walked out, I was detoured away from my homecoming reunion with loved ones who had already crossed over and purposely kept away from my life's review with the Etheric Council. I was lovingly taken to Spirit Hospital where I was wrapped and cocooned in light and nurtured back to health. I was completely empty of self-love and so far away from my Divine eternal nature, that in Earth's time, it took ten years of nourishment and healing to bring me to the stage that I was strong enough to face my life's review and to go over the contract of my life.

Walking up the steps of the Hall of Akashic Records to meet with the Etheric Council, I was very nervous, as this had been my first incarnation and I did not know what to expect. As I walked into the Hall, I began to imagine that the Council was going to come down really hard on me because I chose to exit my human incarnation before its contracted finish. Shaking with fear, I suddenly saw the

Elders appear before me and heard them speak as one. "Hello, lovely Claire. Welcome back. It is so good to see you again. Tell us of your experiences in human form."

Immediately, I launched into a tirade of how hard I tried to make my marriage work and how ill treated I was, validating the reasons as to why I had divorced. Presenting my case like a good lawyer, I spoke about how much I gave when so little was coming back, how I was treated like a servant and what a good mother and wife I had been; as if I was somehow justifying the life that I lived and the reasons that I continually asked God to take my life. The sage Elders listened patiently and let me speak until my discourse came to an end.

One of the wise ones stood, tilted his head and said, "Do you want us to tell you that you lived a worthy life, a life of meaning?" I hesitated, as I was not sure what answer they wished to hear. He continued, "For if you are waiting for a pass or fail, or our condemnation or praise, then, my dear, you will be waiting for eternity. These are your experiences and the only thing that truly matters is what you learned and garnered from this lifetime, and how you feel about yourself."

Upon hearing those words, I felt an enormous weight lift off my shoulders as I understood that I could let go of the burden of defending my time in physical form. It dawned on me that the 'therefore' that I was trying so hard to validate did not matter and was not an issue.

The Elders then said, "So Claire, what did you learn from your lifetime on Earth?"

Taking a deep breath, I replied, "The abuse that I drew to myself in my relationships, because of my low self-worth and denial of who I was, taught me to honour and respect myself and never let anyone diminish me ever again. I learned that one can only be treated like a servant if one allows it. I learned that my capacity to give love freely was not dependent on whether I received love, for the gift was in the giving. Through choosing to bear children, I learned of my enormous capacity to give to another person more than I ever thought possible."

Thinking about my beautiful children, I began to cry. As tears rolled down my cheeks, I added, "And I learned just how strong I was, as I waited for twenty-two years, and until my children were older, before I divorced their father."

Speaking in one voice, the Etheric Council said, "Claire, you have garnered invaluable life's lessons and if you so choose, you will be able to build your next incarnation on these powerful truths."

We then both signed my contract.

Over the past two years, I have gained much information going to Spiritual School and learning all I can in preparation for my next incarnation. I have already put in a request to choose the country, the circumstances and my gender for my next human life. And although my teachers have been very good, my heart holds a very dear spot for my wonderful Teacher Angel Ariel and I am so grateful to her for taking on the responsibility of cleaning up areas of my life and creating such a beautiful world for both of us.

With eternal thanks and love,
Claire Candy

About the Author

As a writer and author, international radio host, inspirational speaker, Reiki Master/Teacher and an Angel Practitioner, Claire Candy Hough helps individuals raise their consciousness and reconnect to the Divine within. She established her business, Angel Healing House, www. angelhealinghouse.com, after her spiritual awakening and Walk-In experience in 2003.

As a healing practitioner, Claire Candy helps her clients transform their lives physically and emotionally through Reiki, a form of energy medicine. As a clairvoyant and intuitive counselor, she marries spiritual knowledge with very grounded and practical ways that people can live truthful lives and shine their authentic light to the world.

After establishing a community of light on the Sunshine Coast in beautiful Queensland, Australia, she and her Twin-Flame, husband Pete, followed the voice of the Divine and moved to the United States in 2008. With her move to the Los Angeles area in 2010, Claire Candy has brought her enthusiasm, passion and joy as she helps others to live authentic lives and manifest their dreams.

Her beautiful channeled book, *Angels of Faith,* was published in 2009 and is based on her two near-death experiences. Claire Candy's beautiful, guided, angel meditation CD, *Letting Go of Concerns and Living in the NOW!,* takes the listener on a wonderful journey with the angels that helps restore peace, balance and calm.

Claire Candy has appeared on television and radio in California and Australia and has designed several transformative workshops including:

The Twin-Flame
Relationship Workshop

A Twin-Flame is the only other person in any space, time or dimension who is the completion of who you are. When brought together, it is the original Divine representation of perfect love. This workshop addresses why you haven't yet drawn this beautiful love to yourself and the important, practical tools that you can consciously focus on to bring such a relationship to you.

"I would recommend Candy's 'Twin Flame Relationship Workshop' to anyone curious about making the right choices in their lives. Candy's presentation clearly demonstrated how our life's story is interrelated to our own belief system. She teaches through examples how each human being is born with an already built-in intuition and, by not honoring this inner wisdom, we can wreak havoc in our personal lives. Candy's approach to her teachings stems from her own personal life experience from her two near-death experiences and the chain of events that followed throughout her life. Her life's teachings have shown me how to appreciate my own unique ability in order to be the change I want to see and to have the courage and clarity to make the right decisions." Renee, Hollywood, CA

Love of Self – Connecting to the Divine Within

This workshop encourages participants to go on an exploration for hidden treasure. This priceless treasure is more valuable and more long-lasting than gold, silver or jewels. It is how to love ourselves. Once we connect with our Divine light within, we will have the clarity, peace and balance to then break the bonds of self-limitation and to reach our highest potential.

"Candy's workshops are extraordinary and transformative. She effortlessly weaves valuable, life-changing information into a highly original, entertaining, practical presentation. Her message of 'Connecting to the Divine Within' is delivered with great enthusiasm, humor and compassion. I came away feeling special and unique, and empowered to pursue my full potential. Thank you, Candy, for your wisdom and your 'Healing from the Heart.' You are truly an Earth angel helping to enlighten others." Peter, Santa Barbara, CA

Near-Death Experiences – An Early Glimpse of Our Journey Back Home

If you have ever wondered about death - and haven't we all at some stage or another? - come along for an enjoyable look at dying. Having had two near-death experiences, Claire Candy remembers vividly her remarkable journey across the veil with the angels and the spiritual insights that she was shown in order to show others to 'not be so afraid of the dark.'

This informative talk will weave Claire Candy's personal near-death experiences with medical and scientific research by eminent doctors in the near-death field like Dr. Elizabeth Kubler-Ross, Dr. Raymond Moody, P.M.H. Atwater and Dr. Kenneth Ring. With humor, great reverence, compassion and love, she is able to make this subject not only enjoyable, but something to look forward to!!

"Candy Hough is an enlightened being, and her journey to that transformation in consciousness through two near-death experiences is shared with warmth, humor and great insight in her presentation entitled, 'Near Death Experiences - An Early Glimpse of Our Journey Back Home.' Candy seamlessly blends well-researched documentation of the near death experience with her own fascinating experience of this life-affirming, life-changing event. You will come away inspired, touched and with a new awareness of that most fascinating of all journeys. It is the best presentation on this topic that I have ever seen."

Reverend Terri Cooper, M.A., MFT, Santa Barbara, CA

CPSIA information can be obtained
at www.ICGtesting.com
Printed in the USA
FSHW011956211021
85666FS